Therese of Lisieux

A Discovery of Love

D1082573

A book in the series
Profiles

Therese of Lisieux

A Discovery of Love

selected spiritual writings

edited and introduced by
Terence Carey, O.C.D.

New City Press

Published in the United States by New City Press
86 Mayflower Avenue, New Rochelle, New York 10801
©1992 New City Press, New York

Text selection throughout based on
Teresa di Lisieux—Nella chiesa sarò l'amore (ed. C. Gennaro, O.C.D.)
©1991 Città Nuova, Rome, Italy

The translations of St. Thérèse's writings have been taken
from the following sources with few minor adjustments:

Story of A Soul, translated by John Clarke, O.C.D.
©1975, 1976 Washington Province of Discalced Carmelite Friars
ICS Publications, 2131 Lincoln Rd., N.E., Washington, D.C. 20002

General Correspondence, Volume One and *Volume Two*,
translated by John Clarke, O.C.D.
©1982, 1988 Washington Province of Discalced Carmelite Friars
ICS Publications, 2131 Lincoln Rd., N.E., Washington, D.C. 20002

Cover design by Nick Cianfarani

Library of Congress Cataloging-in-Publication Data:

Therese of Lisieux : a discovery of love : selected spiritual writings
    / edited and introduced by Terence Carey.

    Includes bibliographical references.
    ISBN 1-56548-014-7
    1. Thérèse, de Lisieux, Saint, 1873-1897.   2. Spiritual life—
Catholic authors.
BX4700.T5T47   1992
282'.092—dc20   92-1614

Printed in the United States of America

CONTENTS

INTRODUCTION

A few minutes after seven o'clock in the evening of September 30, 1897, an unknown Carmelite nun died of tuberculosis in the Carmelite convent at Lisieux in Normandy, France. And yet in her was verified the remark she had made to her sister in a letter dated April 26, 1889: "Yes, Jesus has his preferences; there are, in his garden, fruits which the sun of his love ripens almost in the twinkling of an eye" (Letter 89). In fact, she had not yet reached her twenty-fifth year of age, but she was to be beatified by Pope Pius XI in 1923 and canonized two years later, a quite remarkable feat when one considers the rigorous scrutiny to which the lives and doctrine of candidates for sainthood are subjected by the Church.

Marie-Françoise Thérèse Martin, who took the name of Thérèse of the Child Jesus in religious life, to which she later added "of the Holy Face," was born on January 2, 1873, at 11:30 P.M. Two days later she was baptized in the local parish church dedicated to Our Lady. A neighbor composed a short poem for the occasion:

> Smile now and haste thee to grow
> Happiness beckons thee on,
> Tenderness, loving and careful,
> Eagerly begs thee unclose—
> Smiling, embrace thou the dewdrops,
> Scatter thy perfume afar
> Bud, who at dawn are unfolding,
> Haste to thy splendor as rose!

> (*Story*, Prologue)

The writer could not have known how prophetic his words were.

Her Family

Thérèse was born into a devout Catholic family. The rigorous and dour doctrine of Jansenism was prevalent in France at the time, and the Martin family could not but be subtly affected by it, just as the convent of the Carmelites where Thérèse would later be a nun could not remain immune from its pernicious and unlovely influence. Jansenism saw God as harsh and demanding, more intent on exacting justice than dispensing mercy. There was no place for the sinner at the table of this all-holy master. To approach such an account-keeping Lord and avoid his wrath, one had to border on the angelic. Hence the practice of receiving holy communion only infrequently, and even then with the permission of one's confessor or superior. How ironic, then, that this "delicate flower," Thérèse of the Child Jesus, should be one of the foremost in breaking the tyranny of Jansenism, and should show to the world that God is a loving and merciful Savior, a God who is "slow to anger and rich in mercy." She sums up her attitude in one sentence: "My way is all confidence and love; I don't understand souls who fear a friend so tender" (Letter 226).

Louis Martin, Thérèse's father, was born in Bordeaux. His father was a soldier who campaigned in Spain before being transferred to Alençon in Normandy. It soon became obvious that Louis Martin was not cut out for a military career. A quiet, introspective young man, he lived the Christian life to the full, but there seemed to be no wish on his part to enter the matrimonial state. His mother was becoming concerned that he was still single. It seemed providential, therefore, that she should notice a good Catholic girl among those attending a course for the making of Alençon lace. The young lady in question was Zélie Guerin.

Marie Azélie Guerin was now in her mid-twenties, having been born in December 1831 in Gandelain (Orne). Her father was a former soldier who later became a constable. Her mother was an unlettered peasant and relations between her and Zélie were always strained.

The circumstances of the first meeting of Louis Martin and Zélie Guerin are unclear. Some would have it that Zélie had an inner inspiration, when she saw Louis one day, that this was the man for her. Others suggest that the two mothers played a part in bringing them together. Whatever the circumstances, it seems to have been love at first sight. Scarcely three months after their first meeting they were married on July 13, 1858, at midnight as was the custom then, in the church of Notre Dame in Alençon.

At first they lived as brother and sister, but on the advice of a confessor they decided to start a family. Zélie was to confess later, before the birth of Thérèse, her ninth child: "I love children even to the point of folly, and was born to have some of my own" (*Story*, p. 3). Of the nine children she had, seven were girls and two boys. The boys and two of the girls died at birth or soon afterwards. Despite her many confinements, Zélie carried on her lace business vigorously. So successful was she that she could employ several other people and her husband, Louis, sold his watchmaking business to devote himself to Zélie's trade. It was he who did all the necessary travelling, purchasing and bookkeeping. It is clear that Zélie was a woman of extraordinary ability and profound Christian conviction. Even when her strength was failing due to inoperable breast-cancer, her sister said that she managed her household with the "really incredible and prodigious courage of the strong woman! Adversity does not get her down nor does prosperity make her proud" (*Story*, p. 4).

This, then, was the family into which Thérèse was born. "God was pleased all through my life to surround me with love, and the first memories I have are stamped with smiles and the most tender caresses" (*Story*, p. 17). Her mother would have been happy to nurse the child herself, but in her poor state of health this was not possible. Unable to breast-feed the child—something which the doctor considered essential—Zélie reluctantly fostered out the baby to Rose Taillè who lived in Semallè, some five miles from Alençon. Thérèse remained there for just over a year. The country air suited her and by July 1873 she was a "big baby tanned by the sun." At last, on April 2, 1874, the family rejoiced to have her back at home. At this point the two older girls, Marie and Pauline, were boarders at the Visitation school in Le Mans, where their aunt, Sr. Marie-Dosithèe, kept a vigilant eye on them. It is from their mother's letters to them that we learn most about the early childhood of Thérèse, and Thérèse herself cites these letters extensively in her autobiography. For example, there is a letter dated June 25, 1874, when Thérèse was only a year and a half old: "Your father just installed a swing and Céline's joy knows no bounds. But you should see the little one using it; it's funny to see her trying to conduct herself as a big girl. There's no danger of her letting the rope go. When the swing doesn't go fast enough she cries. We attached her to it with a rope, but in spite of this I'm still uneasy to see her perched so high" (*ibid.*).

Not surprisingly, in a family where the things of the spirit were given their rightful place, Thérèse soon learned that we are in exile here and that heaven is our true home. In a letter of December 5, 1875, from Zélie to Pauline she says: "Baby is a little imp; she'll kiss me and at the same time wish me to die. 'Oh, how I wish you would die, dear little mother!' When I scold her she answers: 'It is because I want you to go to heaven, and you say we must die to get there!' She wishes the same for her father in her outbursts of affection for him" (*ibid.*).

We must not conclude, however, that Thérèse was already a saint at this early stage. Let us hear her mother again: "My little Céline is drawn to the practice of virtue; it's part of her nature; she is candid and has a horror of evil. As for the little imp, one doesn't know how things will go, she is so small, so thoughtless! Her intelligence is superior to Céline's, but she's less gentle and has a stubborn streak in her that is almost invincible; when she says 'no' nothing can make her give in, and one could put her in the cellar a whole day and she'd sleep there rather than say 'yes' "(*Story*, p. 22). But the good example around her, and the loving but firm formation she received in the home soon began to take effect. By March 1877 Zélie could write to Pauline: "The little one will be alright too, for she wouldn't tell a lie for all the gold in the world, and she has a spirit about her which I have not seen in any of you" (*Story*, p. 28). Again she writes: "The little one is our whole happiness. She will be good; one can already see the germ of goodness in her. She speaks only about God and wouldn't miss her prayers for anything" (*ibid.*).

Her Mother's Death

"Ah! how quickly those sunny years passed by, those years of my childhood" (*Story*, p. 29). Brief, indeed, were those sunny years. Thérèse was only four and a half when her mother died on August 28, 1877. This traumatic experience left the child numb: "I don't recall having cried very much, neither did I speak to anyone about the feelings I experienced. I looked and listened in silence" (*Story*, p. 33). Now began the second of the three periods into which she divided her life and the "most painful of the three. . . . This period extends from the age of four and a half to that of fourteen, the time when I found once again my childhood character" (*Story*, p. 34). From being full of life and happiness, she became timid, retiring and hypersensitive. Tears were never far from her eyes; she found the presence of strangers intolerable and it was only in the family circle that she was at ease. Love was not lacking to her: her father idolized her, always calling her his "little queen," and her sisters Marie and Pauline were real mothers to her in their caring and affection.

After the death of Zélie the family moved from Alençon to Lisieux in order to be near Isidore, Zélie's brother, and his family. Soon life assumed a sense of normality for Thérèse, with the mornings devoted to classes with Marie and the afternoons spent in the company of her adored father. It was on one of these afternoon walks that Thérèse entered the chapel of the Carmelite nuns for the first time, and her father explained to her that the nuns were in there behind the grille of the choir. "I was far from thinking at that time that nine years later I would be in their midst" (*Story*, p. 36).

It was in the summer of 1879 or 1880 that there occurred an incident which was to make a deep impression on Thérèse, even if its full significance would be appreciated only many years later. Let us hear her own account of it: "Papa was on a trip for several days and was not expected to return for two more days. It could have been about two or three o'clock in the afternoon; the sun was shining brightly and all nature seemed to be rejoicing. I was alone at the window of an attic which faced the large garden; I was looking straight ahead, my mind occupied with joyful thoughts, when I saw a man dressed exactly like Papa standing in front of the laundry which was just opposite. The man had the same height and walk as Papa, only he was much more stooped. His head was covered with a sort of apron of indistinct color and it hid his face. He wore a hat similar to Papa's. I saw him walking at a regular pace along my little garden. Immediately a feeling of supernatural fright invaded my soul, but in an instant I reflected that surely Papa had returned and was hiding to surprise me; then I called out very loudly: 'Papa! Papa!' my voice trembling with emotion. But the mysterious personage, appearing not to hear, continued his steady pace without even turning around. Following him with my eyes, I saw him go toward the grove which divides the wide path in two, and I waited to see him reappear at the other side of the tall trees, but the prophetic vision had vanished! All this lasted but an instant but was so deeply engraved on my heart that today, after fifteen years, it is as present to me as though I were still seeing the vision before my eyes" (*Story*, pp. 45-46). "Very often . . . I tried to lift the veil which was hiding its meaning from me because I kept in the bottom of my heart the conviction that this vision had a meaning which was one day to be revealed to me. . . . It was indeed Papa, who was bearing on his venerable countenance and white hair the symbol of his glorious trial.* Just as the adorable face of Jesus was veiled during his passion, so the face of his faithful servant had to be veiled in the days of his sufferings in order that

---

* The paralysis which affected M. Martin's mental faculties during the last five years of his life.

it might shine in the heavenly fatherland near its Lord, the eternal Word" (*Story*, pp. 46-47). Thérèse was eight and a half when she began classes in the local Benedictine Abbey school. These school-days, she tells us, were the saddest five years of her life, and it was only the presence of her sister, Céline, that made them bearable. Indeed she says that but for the companionship of Céline she would be sick in a month, a fact that was verified when Céline did actually leave the school. Due to her shyness and sensitivity she did not mix easily with other children, and she had little interest in the games they played. Having been well instructed by her sisters, she was almost always first in her class, despite the fact that she was the youngest. As well as that she was an attractive child, dearly loved by her teachers. All of this combined to make her an object of jealousy to some of her companions, in particular to one girl who was much older and not very intelligent. Thérèse had to pay dearly for her successes.

Pauline's Entry to Carmel

But now one of the great sorrows of her childhood was about to befall her. One day she heard Pauline speaking to Marie about her imminent entry to Carmel. "I didn't know what Carmel was, but I understood that Pauline was going to leave me to enter a convent. I understood, too, she would not wait for me and I was about to lose my second mother!" (*Story*, p. 58). Pauline explained to her the life of Carmel, and she felt that Carmel was the desert where God wanted her to go to hide herself: "It was not the dream of a child led astray but the certitude of a divine call; I wanted to go to Carmel not for Pauline's sake but for Jesus' sake alone" (*ibid.*). She confided her secret to Pauline and later to the mother prioress in the convent. Mother de Gonzague did not discourage her but she told her that she would have to wait until she was sixteen.

Pauline entered Carmel on October 2, 1882. This shattering experience had a great bearing on Thérèse's illness which now began to manifest itself. Toward the end of the year, she began to have constant headaches. This lasted until Easter 1883. One evening, while her father and her two sisters, Marie and Léonie, were away in Paris and Céline and Thérèse were staying with their aunt, she was seized with a strange trembling as she prepared for bed. The doctor did not specify the nature of the illness, but he said it was serious and one that had never attacked a child as young as Thérèse. However, she was able to attend Pauline's taking of the habit, but the next day she had another attack from which she was not expected to recover: "I can't describe this strange sickness, but I'm now convinced that it was the work of the devil" (*Story*, p. 62).

Heaven was stormed for her recovery. Her father sent an offering to the shrine of Our Lady of Victories in Paris for a novena of Masses for her cure. During the novena, on the feast of Pentecost 1883, Marie, Léonie and Céline were with her in the sick-room, and they turned in prayer to the statue of the Blessed Virgin which was in the room. Thérèse, too, prayed to the Mother of God to take pity on her: "All of a sudden the Blessed Virgin appeared beautiful to me, so beautiful that never had I seen anything so attractive; her face was suffused with an ineffable benevolence and tenderness, but what penetrated to the very depths of my soul was the 'ravishing smile of the Virgin Mary.' At that instant, all my pain disappeared, and two large tears glistened on my eye-lashes, and flowed down my cheeks silently, but they were tears of unmixed joy" (*Story*, pp. 65-66).

One of the things that Thérèse enjoyed most as a child was reading, and this attraction lasted until her entry to Carmel. "I didn't always understand the realities of life," she tells us, when she was reading certain tales of chivalry, "but soon God made me feel that true glory is that which will last eternally, and to reach it, it isn't necessary to perform striking works but to hide oneself and practice virtue in such a way that the left hand knows not what the right is doing" (*Story*, p. 72). Joan of Arc had a special attraction for her, and she felt something of the burning zeal of the French heroine. "Then I received a grace which I have always looked upon as one of the greatest of my life. . . . I didn't think then that one had to suffer very much to reach sanctity, but God was not long in showing me this was so and sending me the trials I have already mentioned" (*ibid.*).

Her first visit back to Alençon was three months after her cure. She was happy to visit her mother's grave, but the visit also produced some salutary lessons from their friends there: "The friends we had there were too worldly; they knew too well how to ally the joys of this earth to the service of God. They didn't think of death enough" (*Story*, p. 73). Later, when she was a nun, she would return in spirit to the enchanting days she passed during her visit to Alençon, but she concluded: "And I see that all is vanity and vexation of spirit under the sun (Wis 4:12), that the only good is to love God with all one's heart and to be poor in spirit here on earth" (*ibid.*).

Her first communion was one of the most memorable events of her young life. "The time of my first communion remains engraved in my heart as a memory without clouds. It seems to me I could not have been better disposed to receive him than I was" (*ibid.*). Indeed, her preparation had begun four years previously when Céline was making her first communion. Now, however, she increased her fervent acts and aspirations. At last "the beautiful day" arrived: "Ah! how sweet was that first kiss of Jesus! It was a kiss of love; I felt I was loved, and I said: 'I love you, and I give myself to you forever!' " (*Story*, p. 77).

It was while preparing for her second communion one year later that she was assailed by scruples, and this torture was to continue for a year and half. Her sister Marie was endlessly patient in listening to her daily litany of these scruples, while Thérèse could not stop crying during the recitation. Another trial for her at this time was that Cèline left the Abbey school, having finished her studies. Obliged to attend classes without her inseparable companion, Thérèse soon became ill and had to be withdrawn from the school and sent for private tuition to Mme. Papineau. The year 1886 brought more suffering with the entry of Marie to Carmel, Marie who was her greatest support and who "knew . . . everything that went on in my soul" (*Story*, p. 88). Bereft of her confidante, she turned to heaven to the "four angels who had preceded me there" (*Story*, p. 93). "The answer was not long in coming, for soon peace came to inundate my soul with its delightful waves, and I knew that if I was loved on earth, I was also loved in heaven" (*ibid.*).

From the beginning of her life Thérèse was a sensitive and nervous child. Her mother wrote to Pauline on May 21, 1876: "She becomes emotional very easily." Again she said that Thérèse "gets into frightful tantrums" and "she's a nervous child" (*Story*, p. 23). This condition was compounded with the death of her mother and the entry of Pauline and Marie to Carmel. She admits that at the age of thirteen she was really unbearable because of her extreme touchiness. Not only did she cry if she offended someone she loved, but she even cried again for having cried. It would require a miracle to correct this trait in her character. The miracle happened after Midnight Mass of Christmas 1886. It had always been the custom to leave her presents in her shoes in the chimney-corner, and after Midnight Mass she would draw them out with shrieks of delight to the great joy of her father. On this particular evening, just as she went upstairs to remove her hat, she overheard her father saying that fortunately this would be the last time she would go through the ritual. He felt that she should have outgrown the childish custom by now. Thérèse excuses her father on the grounds that he was tired after the Midnight Mass. Céline, seeing the tears starting in Thérèse's eyes, urged her not to go down immediately. But the miracle occurred: Thérèse was able to go down and behave as if she had heard nothing. "Thérèse had discovered once again the strength of soul she had lost at the age of four and a half, and she was to preserve it forever" (*Story*, p. 98). It was the start of the third period of her life "the most beautiful and the most filled with graces from heaven" (*ibid.*). "Since that night I have never been defeated in any combat, but rather walked from victory to victory" (*Story*, p. 97).

Now, she tells us, charity entered her soul. One Sunday, looking at a picture of our Lord on the cross, she was struck by the blood flowing from one of the divine hands. It caused her great sorrow that there was no one to gather up this blood, and she resolved to remain in spirit at the foot of the cross to receive "this divine dew" and to pour it out on souls. The cry of our Lord on the cross, "I thirst," sounded continually in her heart and she felt consumed with a thirst for souls.

Her spiritual life was nurtured by assiduous reading of the *Imitation of Christ*, a book she knew almost by heart. But now another book, which had been lent to her father by the Carmelites, came into her hands. This was Abbé Arminjon's conferences on the end of the world and the mysteries of the future life. The reading of this book was "one of the greatest graces in my life. . . . All the great truths of religion, the mysteries of eternity, plunged my soul into a state of joy not of this earth. I experienced already what God reserved for those who love him (not with the eye but with the heart), and seeing the eternal rewards had no proportion to life's small sacrifices, I wanted to love, to love Jesus with a passion, giving him a thousand proofs of my love while it was possible" (*Story*, p. 102).

Thérèse's Trials to Enter Carmel

More and more she felt drawn to Carmel. She had the support of Pauline but Marie tried to cool her ardor. When she told Céline of her desire the latter became the confidante of all her struggles and sufferings. But the greatest problem was to tell her father. She was only fourteen and a half and her father idolized her. How would he react to her entering Carmel? Finally, she chose the feast of Pentecost 1887 to break the news to him. She soon convinced him that her desire was God's will and he cried out that God was giving him a great honor in asking his children from him. Pointing to some little white flowers "like lilies in miniature" on a low wall of the garden, he plucked one of them and gave it to her, explaining that God had brought it into being and preserved it to that very day. Thérèse could see her own life symbolized in this little flower which her father plucked by the roots so that it could be transferred to another soil.

The way seemed now clear for her entry to Carmel, but such was not to be. Her uncle Isidore strenuously opposed her desire on the grounds of age, and said that only a miracle could make him change his mind. But the miracle happened. The next time she saw him he told her that she was a little flower that God wanted to gather, and he would no longer oppose it. Now another and more formidable obstacle materialized in the person of the ecclesiastical superior of the convent, Canon Delatroëtte. He was adamant that she should not enter until she was twenty-one. However, he pointed out that he was only the bishop's delegate, and he assured her that if the bishop gave his consent there would be no problem on his part. So she had to face the bishop of Bayeux. The bishop received her kindly but would not make a decision without consulting the ecclesiastical superior of the convent. He told her he would let her have his reply in due course. In the meantime, Louis Martin had decided to go to Rome for the jubilee of Pope Leo XIII, taking his daughters Céline and Thérèse with him. Thérèse resolved that she would ask the Holy Father in person for permission to enter Carmel at the age of fifteen.

She describes in some detail her journey to the Eternal City; Switzerland "with its mountains whose summits were lost in the clouds, its graceful waterfalls gushing forth in a thousand different ways, its deep valleys literally covered with gigantic ferns and scarlet heather"; Milan, where the bishop of Bayeux, who was leading the pilgrimage, offered Mass on the tomb of St. Charles while "we were behind the altar with Papa, resting our heads on the tomb enshrining his body which was clothed in its pontifical robes"; Venice, where she saw the underground cells and dungeons and "I imagined myself living back in the days of the martyrs and would have willingly remained there in order to imitate them"; Padua, "where we venerated the tongue of St. Anthony," and then Bologna, "where we saw St. Catherine who retains the imprint of the kiss of the Infant Jesus" (*Story,* pp. 125-28). But it was Loreto with its "Holy House" that gave her the greatest consolation. There she and Céline were able to receive holy communion in the Santa Casa.

She has left us the principal impressions she retained from the visit to Rome. The Colosseum had a particular attraction for her, and she was not satisfied until she found the spot, marked by a cross, where the martyrs fought. Daringly, she and Céline got to the place: "My heart was beating hard when my lips touched the dust stained with the blood of the first Christians. I asked for the grace of being a martyr for Jesus and felt that my prayer was answered" (*Story*, p. 131). The Catacombs also made a deep impression on her, and she found the tomb of St. Cecilia and took some earth which was sanctified by her presence: "She became my saint of predilection, my intimate confidante" (*ibid.*). She visited the church of St. Agnes, her "childhood friend," and collected a small piece of red stone which had detached itself from a rich mosaic as a relic of the saint.

Six days were spent visiting the principal attractions of the city, and on the seventh day they had their audience with Pope Leo XIII, the chief purpose of her journey as far as Thérèse was concerned. She describes her preparation for the audience and the scene in the pontifical apartment, although she admits that she saw it only in general because her only preoccupation was the Holy Father. She was determined to speak, but just as her turn to approach the pope came it was announced that it was forbidden to address the Holy Father. She turned to Céline who uttered just one word: "Speak!" And she did speak: "Most Holy Father, I have a great favor to ask you. . . . Holy Father, in honor of your jubilee, permit me to enter Carmel at the age of fifteen!" (*Story*, p. 134). The pope was very gentle with her but did not grant her request. His words were: "Go . . . go . . . You will enter if God wills it" (*Story*, p. 135).

For some time she had offered herself to the Child Jesus as his little plaything. Now Jesus pierced his little toy to see what was inside, and being content with the discovery he let it fall to the ground and went to sleep. The sadness of her soul did not prevent her from taking a lively interest in the other places they visited: Naples, Assisi and Florence, Pisa and Genoa. Despite the beauty of the scenery and the sight of all these things that she was seeing for the first and last time "it was without regret I saw them disappear, for my heart longed for other marvels. I had contemplated earthly beauties long enough; those of heaven were the object of its desires and to win them for souls I was willing to become a prisoner!" (*Story*, p. 141).

Her Entry to Carmel   Discipline of secrecy.

On her return to Lisieux, Pauline urged her to write to the bishop, reminding him of his promise to let her have his answer. Christmas passed with no reply forthcoming, and then on New Year's Day, 1888, she was informed by Mother Marie de Gonzague that the bishop had written to the convent on December 28 giving his permission, but the community had decided to postpone her entry until after Lent, no doubt to spare her the extra sacrifices that are customary in Carmelite convents during this penitential season. She was disappointed, but she spent the time fruitfully in trying to break her will "always so ready to impose itself on others," in rendering little services without any recognition, etc. "It was through the practice of these nothings that I prepared myself to become the fiancée of Jesus" (*Story*, pp. 144-45).

April 9, 1888, was the day set for her entry. "My heart was beating so violently it seemed impossible to walk when they signaled for me to come to the enclosure door. I advanced, however, asking myself whether I was going to die because of the beating of my heart! Ah! what a moment that was! One would have to experience it to know what it is" (*Story*, p. 147). She knelt for her father's blessing and he too, went on his knees while giving it, tears flowing down his cheeks. Moments later, she was inside the doors of the enclosure where her sisters waited to embrace her. "My desires were at last accomplished; my soul experienced a peace so sweet, so deep, it would be impossible to express it" (*Story*, p. 148), and seven years later she would say that this inner peace had never left her, even in the midst of the greatest trials.

Everything about Carmel thrilled her. She tells us that she had not a single illusion when she entered Carmel. She found it exactly as she had imagined it; no sacrifice astonished her, and thorns were not lacking to her first steps in the convent: "Yes, suffering opened wide its arms to me and I threw myself into them with love" (*Story*, p. 149). She had come to save souls and especially to pray for priests, which was one of the principal motives for the foundation of the first Carmelite convent in Avila, Spain, by St. Teresa of Avila. Jesus made Thérèse understand that it was through suffering that he would give her souls. This attraction for suffering increased in proportion to the suffering itself. God took her at her word, and sent her many trials. On the last day of her life she could say: "Never would I have believed it was possible to suffer so much!

Never! I cannot explain this except by the ardent desires I have to save souls" (*Last Conversations*, p. 205).

In what did these sufferings consist? We saw some of the sorrows of her childhood, but now she was entering a new and more demanding phase of her life. Thérèse had been accustomed to a fairly comfortable lifestyle. She admits that when she was at home "I wasn't accustomed to doing things for myself. Céline tidied up the room in which we slept, and I myself didn't do any housework whatsoever" (*Story*, p. 97), although she did make some effort after Marie had entered Carmel. In Carmel she had to accept her share of the community chores; she had to be content with the clothing, food, heating (or lack of it), early rising and long hours of work and prayer. All of this might not make great demands on a grown woman accustomed to working in the family before her entry, but Thérèse was still only a teenager, and a delicately nurtured one at that.

In a Carmelite convent, the novices spend a good deal of time in the company of the novice mistress. It was particularly unfortunate for Thérèse, then, that she did not relate well with the novice mistress for two years. One of her companion novices was difficult to get on with. The prioress, Mother Marie de Gonzague, treated her with severity: "God permitted that she was very severe without her even being aware of it. I was unable to meet her without having to kiss the floor" * (*Story*, p. 150). There was, especially, the problem of her own sisters: "I didn't come to Carmel to live with my sisters but to answer Jesus' call. Ah! I really felt in advance that this living with one's own sisters had to be the cause of continual suffering when one wishes to grant nothing to one's natural inclination" (*Story*, p. 216). The fact that she worked with Pauline in the refectory added to the problem: "How I suffered then, dear Mother," she says, addressing Pauline, "I could not open my heart to you and it was as though you knew me no longer" (*Story*, p. 160; *Last Conversations*, p. 96). This was because she wished to observe the strict rule of silence prescribed by the Carmelite Rule.

All of this, however, was external, and could not be compared with the interior trials she underwent. "Spiritual aridity was my daily bread" (*Story*, p. 157). Few have described what prayer is as simply but profoundly as she: "For me, prayer is an aspiration of the heart, it is a simple glance directed to heaven, it is a cry of gratitude and love in the midst of trial as well as joy; finally, it is something great, supernatural, which

---

* It was the custom in the convent to kiss the floor when one had committed a fault.

expands my soul and unites me to Jesus" (*Story*, p. 242). From this one would think that the two hours of prayer enjoined by the Carmelite Rule would be periods of intense happiness and consolation, and yet she tells us that sometimes her mind is in such great aridity that it is impossible to draw forth one single thought to unite her with God. Indeed, she even goes to sleep during her prayer time.

Probably the greatest exterior trial of her life was the illness of her father. Thérèse had scarcely entered Carmel when the first signs of mental impairment began to manifest themselves in her father. He began to rave, to suffer hallucinations and to wander off, so that he had to be continually watched. Eventually he was admitted to a mental hospital in Caen: "Ah! that day, I didn't say I was able to suffer more! Words cannot express our anguish, and I'm not going to attempt to describe it. . . . My desire for suffering was answered, and yet my attraction for it did not diminish" (*Story*, p. 157). Added to the trial of knowing that her father was drinking the "most bitter and humiliating of all chalices" (*Story*, p. 156) was the fact that some people were suggesting that it was the entry of his youngest daughter to Carmel that had sparked off the illness. Even in the community, some of the Sisters were lacking in delicacy in their attitude and remarks regarding M. Martin's condition. This cross was to last, with some remission, until his death on July 29, 1894.

Before Easter 1896, Thérèse "was enjoying such a living faith, such a clear faith, that the thought of heaven made up all my happiness, and I was unable to believe that there were really impious people who had no faith" (*Story*, p. 211). But then during the Easter season, Jesus permitted her soul to be invaded by the thickest darkness, so that "the thought of heaven, up until then so sweet to me" was "no longer anything but the cause of struggle and torment. This trial was to last not a few days or a few weeks, it was not to be extinguished until the hour set by God himself and this hour has not yet come" (*Story*, pp. 211-12). There were times when she felt she heard mocking voices trying to get her to despair about even the existence of heaven, and telling her that nothing awaited her after death but a night of nothingness. Although she may have appeared to others as if the veil of faith was already torn aside to give her vision, for her "it is no longer a veil . . . it is a wall which reaches right up to the heavens and covers the starry firmament" (*Story*, p. 214).

Thérèse received the habit on January 10, 1889. She even had the joy of having her father present, despite his illness: "This was really his day of triumph and it was to be his last celebration on this earth" (*Story*, p.

155). She had always loved snow, and it was her wish that there would be snow on the day of her clothing, even though the weather was particularly mild at the time. Imagine her joy when she entered the enclosure after the ceremony to find the garden "white like me." Her profession should have taken place one year later, but it was postponed for eight months. At last, on September 8, 1890, "the beautiful day of my wedding arrived" (*Story*, p. 166). But on the eve of the ceremony, a further trial beset her; she had doubts about her vocation. She called the novice mistress out of the choir to tell her that she feared she was deceiving the community. Fortunately the novice mistress was a woman of considerable experience and was able to assure Thérèse that she had, indeed, a vocation. Not content, however, with this reassurance, she also confided in the prioress. Mother Marie de Gonzague only laughed at her doubts. "Everything was little that day except the graces and the peace I received, and the peaceful joy I experienced in the evening when gazing at the stars shining in the firmament and thinking that soon this beautiful heaven would open up to my ravished eyes, and I would be able to unite myself to my spouse in the bosom of eternal happiness" (*Story*, p. 167).

After her profession, the life of Thérèse seemed just like that of any other member of the community. But on February 20, 1893, her sister, Mother Agnes of Jesus, was elected prioress, and Thérèse could later tell her: "O Mother, it was especially since the blessed day of your election that I have flown in the ways of love" (*Story*, p. 174). Mother Agnes, according to custom, appointed Mother Marie de Gonzague as novice mistress, but she gave her Thérèse as assistant, a delicate position given the unpredictable character of Mother de Gonzague. It is interesting to note how one of the members of the community describes Thérèse at this time:

"Tall and robust, childlike, with a tone of voice and expression to match, hiding the wisdom, perfection and discernment of a fifty-year-old. She is always composed, and in perfect control of herself in everything and with everyone. An innocent little thing to whom you would give communion without confession, but her head is full of tricks to play on whoever she pleases. A mystic, a comic, she has everything going for her—she knows how to make you weep with devotion or die with laughter at recreation."*

---

* Cf. Gaucher, G., *The Spiritual Journey of St. Thérèse*, tr. Anne Marie Brennan, O.C.D. (London: Darton, Longman & Todd), p. 126.

Longing For Sanctity

M. Martin died on July 29, 1894, and now the way was clear for Céline to join her sisters in Carmel. Some members of the community were hesitant to allow a fourth member of the same family to enter the convent, but Thérèse prayed that this opposition would evaporate. And her prayer was answered. The sister who had most objected to the entry now assured Thérèse that she no longer opposed the move. Now, Thérèse would say, all her earthly desires were fulfilled. "You know, Mother, I have always wanted to be a saint" (*Story*, p. 207). She felt that this was a wish inspired by Jesus and he never gave inspirations incapable of fulfillment. The problem was that when she compared herself with the saints they seemed like mountains with their summits lost in the clouds, while she was an obscure grain of sand trampled underfoot by the passers-by. How was she to achieve this lofty goal, little as she was? "I wanted to seek out a means of going to heaven by a little way, a way that is very straight, very short, and totally new" (*ibid.*). As always, she looked to scripture for a solution, and her eye fell on the passage from Proverbs 9:4: "Whoever is a little one, let him come to me." She had found what she was looking for. She had no need to grow up, but rather to remain little and become so more and more. In the early part of her religious life Thérèse had thought of sanctity as something to be "won at the point of the sword," something that could be *acquired* by accumulating merit. But as she progressed it was given to her to understand that "merit does not consist in doing or giving much, but in *receiving*, in loving much" (Letter 121). Now there was no longer question of relying on her own efforts: "Jesus is teaching her [Thérèse] to play at the bank of love or rather, he plays for her and does not tell her how he goes about it, for that is his affair and not Thérèse's. What she must do is abandon herself, surrender herself, without keeping anything, not even the joy of knowing how much the bank is returning to her" (Letter 142). Here we have that complete abandonment to Jesus, allowing herself to be carried by him, totally trusting as a little child trusts its father. Now she realized that sanctity is sheer gift, and the condition for receiving it is total availability. It is always the Divine Eagle who must carry the little bird to the heights.

Thérèse entered Carmel "not for love of Pauline but for love of Jesus." As she progressed, her desires to love God more increased, but she feared that her faults might be an obstacle to that love. At the retreat the year after her profession, the director, Fr. Alexis Prou, assured her that her faults caused God no pain. This reassurance launched her full sail upon the waves of confidence and love. The entry of Céline to Carmel satisfied her one remaining earthly desire, "And now I have no other desire except to love Jesus unto folly . . . neither do I desire any longer suffering or death, and still I love them both; it is love alone that attracts me" (*Story*, p. 178). But the love she means is not just her human love for Jesus. At her profession she had asked for "infinite love without any limits other than yourself; love which is no longer I but you, my Jesus" (*Story*, p. 275). How could she love God as God loved her? "For me to love you as you love me, I would have to borrow your own love, and then only would I be at rest" (*Story*, p. 256). This longing to love Jesus as he deserved to be loved came to a climax on Sunday, June 9, 1895, the feast of the Most Holy Trinity. She was inspired to offer herself as a sacrificial victim to Merciful Love. She had been thinking of those souls who offer themselves as victims to God's justice in order to divert and bring down on themselves the punishments reserved for the guilty ones. The year before, the story of Sr. Marie-Anne, a Carmelite of Luçon, who had offered herself as a victim of divine justice, was read in the refectory. Thérèse always thought of God in terms of mercy, "and through it I contemplate and adore the other divine perfections" (*Story*, p. 180). "If your justice loves to release itself . . . how much more does your merciful love desire to set souls on fire since your mercy reaches to the heavens. O my Jesus, let me be this happy victim; consume your holocaust with the fire of your divine love" (*Story*, p. 181). Mother Agnes was the prioress at the time, and Thérèse asked for and received permission to make this offering. "Since that happy day, it seems to me that love penetrates and surrounds me, that at each moment this merciful love renews me, purifying my soul and leaving no trace of sin within it, and I need have no fear of purgatory" (*ibid.*). In seeing mercy as encompassing justice, Thérèse was reechoing the teaching of the Old Testament, as we see in the encyclical of Pope John Paul II, *Dives in Misericordia*, where he says: "Mercy is in a certain sense contrasted with God's justice, and in many cases is shown to be not only more powerful than that justice but also more profound. . . . Love, so to speak, conditions justice and, in the final analysis, justice serves love. The primacy and superiority of love vís-à-vís justice—this is a mark of the whole of revelation—are revealed precisely through mercy" (n. 4).

Her Vocation to Love

As her faith in God's merciful love grew, it became a "veritable martyrdom" for her not to be able to satisfy her "immense desires." She was no longer content to be a Carmelite, a spouse, a mother to souls. She wanted to experience all vocations in their fullness. Opening the New Testament at random, her eyes lit upon St. Paul's First Letter to the Corinthians. The "more excellent way" was charity: "Charity gave me the key to my vocation. . . . I understood that love comprised all vocations, that love was everything, that it embraced all times and all places. . . . In a word, that it was eternal!" (*Story*, p. 194). But was she, perhaps, aiming for something beyond her ability? "I am only a child, powerless and weak, and yet it is my weakness that gives me the boldness of offering myself as victim of your love, O Jesus! . . . Love has chosen me as a holocaust, me, a weak and imperfect creature. . . . Yes, in order that love be fully satisfied, it is necessary that it lower itself, and that it lower itself to nothingness and transform this nothingness into fire" (*Story*, p. 195). So here is the answer: to be totally at God's disposal and he will work the impossible.

On January 27, 1897, Thérèse wrote to Brother Simeon, a friend of the Martin family in Rome: "I believe my course here below will not be long" (Letter 218). She was aware that her strength was ebbing. Merciful Love was about to consume its holocaust. During the night of April 2-3, 1896, she had suffered her first hemoptysis. Although she had some remission for about a year, after Lent 1897 the illness took complete control. The remedies of the period have been described as "ineffectual barbarities"— blistering: a cataplasm bound round the chest sometimes for hours at a time to raise enormous blisters, which were then burst in the hope of relieving the lungs; cautery, sometimes on five hundred different spots at one sitting. Added to this were the other effects of tuberculosis for which there was no remedy at the time: death by thirst and suffocation. And then a side-effect of the illness: gangrene of the intestines. Such was the intensity of her pain that she confessed: "If I didn't have faith I should have killed myself without a moment's hesitation" (*Last Conversations*, p. 196). By April 4 she was having digestive troubles and a daily fever. As the days went by there was vomiting, acute chest pains and frequent coughing up of blood. Progressively she had to renounce the community exercises: recreations, chanted office, common duties. On May 18 she was relieved of all work.

Thérèse's Mission

As her life drew to its close, Thérèse became increasingly aware of her mission: "I feel especially that my mission is about to begin, my mission of making God loved as I love him, of giving my little way to souls. If God answers my desires, my heaven will be spent on earth until the end of time. . . . I can't rest as long as there are souls to be saved" (*Last Conversations*, p. 102). During her last days she begged her sisters to make known her "sufferings," because she was convinced that her "mission" would never be understood except in the light of her sufferings. Then she could be a source of inspiration and strength to others.

On the very last day of her life Thérèse summed up in one line the guiding principle of her life: "Yes, it seems to me I never sought anything but the truth; yes, I have understood humility of heart. . . . It seems to me I'm humble" (*Last Conversations*, p. 205). It was the great foundress of the Teresian Carmel who said: "Humility is truth." Thérèse had grasped this at an early stage. For love of truth she was prepared to take a stand when necessary, as when she challenged one of the novices about her over-dependence on the prioress. During her last illness it was suggested that she should make some edifying remark to the doctor, but she would have none of it: "Ah! little Mother, this isn't my little style. Let Doctor de Cornière think what he wants. I love only simplicity; I have a horror of 'pretense.' I assure you that to do what you want would be bad on my part" (*Last Conversations*, p. 77).

The "Divine Thief" was already in the sick-room, ready to bear away his prey. After the doctor's visit on September 29, 1897, Thérèse asked the prioress: "Is it today, Mother?" and the prioress answered: "Yes, my little child." In fact, her agony was to last another day, and shortly after seven o'clock in the evening, looking at her crucifix she said: "Oh! I love him! . . . My God . . . I love you! . . ." Now was fulfilled her desire, expressed in her Act of Oblation to Merciful Love:

> May this martyrdom,
> after having prepared me to appear before you,
> finally cause me to die
> and may my soul take its flight without any delay
> into the eternal embrace of your merciful love.

(*Story*, p. 277)

Some Lessons from Thérèse's Teaching

St. Thérèse has taught us many lessons for the spiritual life, but here I wish merely to indicate some of them. One of fundamental importance is that we should read the scriptures assiduously where, she tells us, "a single word opens up infinite horizons to my soul, perfection seems easy." Again she says: "I have only to cast a glance in the gospels and immediately I breathe in the perfumes of Jesus' life. . . . In them I find what is necessary for my poor little soul. I am constantly discovering in them new lights, hidden and mysterious meanings" (*Story*, p. 179). There is no human life that does not have suffering of some kind in it, and usually we find it difficult to accept these trials or to see any meaning in them. Thérèse points out that suffering is really a gift from God when it is accepted, indeed welcomed, with love. It is worthy of note that several of the ideas we find in Vatican Council II are already there in the writings of the saint. For example when she says that we must not "say unlikely things or things we don't know anything about" (*Last Conversations*, p. 161) when speaking of Our Lady, there is a clear anticipation of the teaching of *Lumen Gentium* when it says: "But it [the sacred synod] strongly urges theologians and preachers of the word of God to be careful to refrain as much from all false exaggeration as from too summary an attitude in considering the special dignity of the Mother of God" (n. 67). Thérèse, in fact, liked to think of the Blessed Virgin, and indeed the Holy Family, as "ordinary," so that we could imitate them. She would certainly applaud the Council for telling us that "true devotion" leads us "to a filial love toward our Mother and to the imitation of her virtues" (n. 67). Has she not said: "Let the priests, then, show us practicable virtues! It's good to speak of her privileges, but it's necessary above all that we can imitate her. She prefers imitation to admiration" (*Last Conversations*, p. 166).

Even a cursory acquaintance with the life and teaching of St. Thérèse will show that love is central to all her doctrine. We saw earlier how she discovered her vocation to be love in the heart of the Church from her reading of St. Paul's First Letter to the Corinthians. We have prepared this anthology from the writings of the saint to show how her life can be built round this one idea of love. It is significant that the last word Thérèse wrote in Manuscripts A, B and C was "Love," and her last words on earth were: "My God . . . I love you! . . ."

It is, of course, as the saint of the "little way" that St. Thérèse is best known. She was insistent that her teaching was for "little souls." She never wished to have extraordinary graces or experiences because this would prevent the "ordinary" Christian from following her "little way." It is interesting to note that Vatican Council II brought to the fore something which seemed to have been forgotten, namely that all are called to holiness: "The Lord Jesus, divine teacher and model of all perfection, preached holiness of life . . . to each and every one of his disciples without distinction. . . . It is therefore quite clear that all Christians in any state or walk of life are called to the fullness of the Christian life and to the perfection of love" (*Lumen Gentium*, n. 40). Thérèse is our model for achieving this perfection. Although there is great depth in her writings— as she said about sacred scripture, we can say about her writings that we are "always finding hidden and mysterious meanings there—yet we are reassured that her teaching works, because she speaks from lived experience and not from a merely theoretical standpoint. Bernard Bro, O.P., has said very beautifully that Thérèse has "democratized" holiness: "What matters is that what was previously reserved for privileged beings like Bernard of Clairvaux, Ignatius Loyola or John of the Cross, we now find being offered to everyone: the opportunity of triumphing over the anguish of our fate, of triumphing over fear of loneliness in the face of uncertainty over the future and death. And Thérèse it is who reveals the secrets of this democratization of the 'dark night of the soul' to us. According to her, within us we each have an explosive, infinite strength capable of conquering every fear. This strength exists in each of us. . . . There is only one condition on which benefiting from this infinite strength depends: that of accepting the truth about our incapacity and, because of this, of choosing the path of trusting to the last."*

Terence Carey, O.C.D.

---

* Bro, B., O.P., *The Little Way; The Spirituality of Thérèse of Lisieux*, tr. Alan Neame (London: Darton, Longman & Todd, 1979), p. 13.

SOURCES

One evening at the beginning of 1895, the three sisters, Marie, Pauline and Thérèse Martin, all now Carmelite nuns, were chatting together during the recreation period in the convent and Thérèse was recounting some of the incidents of her childhood. Since Marie and Pauline were older than Thérèse, the events she was recalling would have been familiar to the two sisters, but it was good to hear Thérèse's version of them. Marie was so taken by what Thérèse was telling them that she turned to Pauline, who was now known as Mother Agnes of Jesus and was prioress of the convent, and asked her to get Thérèse to put these childhood memories in writing, adding: "What pleasure this would give us!" This was the origin of the book that was published a year after the saint's death under the title *Story of a Soul* (*Story* in references). The reader must bear in mind the purpose of the writer—to give pleasure to her sisters, its intended readers, the family circle—and the cultural context in which it was written. When Thérèse was writing, she did not envision a wider public: it was only in the last months of her life that she foresaw that her mission would begin only with her death, and that her writing would have an important place in that mission. Once she realized that her teaching could be useful to souls she directed her sister Pauline to undertake the editing and publishing of the work: "After my death, you mustn't speak to anyone about my manuscript before it is published; you must speak about it only to mother prioress" (Mother Marie was now prioress once again). "If you act otherwise, the devil will make use of more than one trap to hinder the work of God, a very important work" (*Last Conversations,* p. 126). Pauline accepted the task and edited the text fairly liberally, omitting some words or phrases which she thought might be misunderstood outside the convent, but the content of the writing was substantially unaltered.

Story of a Soul as it was published is made up of three distinct sections, now generally referred to as Manuscripts A, B and C. Manuscript A is the one addressed to Pauline as a family souvenir. As we saw above, Thérèse was asked for these childhood memories early in 1895. She wrote only in her spare time, and eventually presented the copybook to Mother

Agnes for her feast-day on January 20, 1896. Mother Agnes was too busy with her duties as prioress to read the document at the time, and it was only after the election of Mother Marie de Gonzague on March 21 of the same year that she was free. Having read the text, Pauline noted that Thérèse had complied with her request in giving her childhood recollections, but she had said very little about her time in religious life. In fact, at the end of the text Thérèse said: "You will forgive me for having abridged my religious life so much" (*Story*, p. 181). Mother Agnes thought it a pity that Thérèse had not given her thoughts on religious life, so she approached the prioress, asking her to get Thérèse to fill out her account of her time in Carmel. The excuse Mother Agnes used for making her request was that "you will not be able to obtain much information to write her circular (obituary notice) after her death, for there is almost nothing in it about her religious life." The purpose of this manuscript, then, was to give Mother de Gonzague some information which could be useful in the circular, but it was never intended for publication. This section of *Story of a Soul* is referred to as Manuscript C. Manuscript B was the result of a request made to Thérèse by her sister, Marie (Sr. Marie of the Sacred Heart), that she would put in writing her little doctrine. This is now chapter IX of *Story of a Soul*.

A sequel to *Story of a Soul* is the *Last Conversations of St. Thérèse*. During her last illness, her sisters, especially Mother Agnes, spent a lot of time with her. They already knew something of her deep interior life, and they wanted as many insights into it as possible while she was still with them. Besides, natural family ties would dictate that they cherish anything she might say in these final days of her life. Lovers of St. Thérèse will be grateful to them for preserving so many gems of spirituality.

Story of a Soul was not intended to be an autobiography in the ordinary sense of that term. Indeed Thérèse herself said it was not "my life properly so called that I am going to write; it is my thoughts on the graces God deigned to grant me." Not surprisingly, then, there are many gaps in the account. Many of these lacunae can be filled by reference to the *Letters* (L) written either by Thérèse herself, written to her or in which there is reference to her. These have been published in two volumes.

To complete the primary sources for a knowledge of the spirituality of the saint, one would need to read her *Plays* and *Poems*. These are of no great literary value, but they do enshrine many of the ideas expressed elsewhere.

Thérèse
of
Lisieux

Spiritual
Writings

PERIOD ONE

The Discovery of Love

January 1873–April 1888

Thérèse of Lisieux was twenty-two when she wrote the *Story of a Soul*, which she tells us is not "my life properly so called . . . it is my thoughts on the graces God deigned to grant me" (*Story*, p. 15). As she wrote, past and present blended for Thérèse, and she was deeply conscious of how God had been leading and directing her whole life. The very fact that she had been able to choose God was seen as a gratuitous gift, "without any merit on my part" (*Story*, p. 256).

When we speak, then, of the "discovery of love," we are referring to the beginning of her life and how she came to know God and to receive her vocation to the Carmelite life. We have not yet reached the stage where she makes her great discovery of her vocation to love in the heart of the Church.

In the life of Thérèse, as in any human life, there are human and divine elements which combine to form the person. She tells us that God willed that she be "born in a holy soil." It was in her devout Catholic family that she first learned about heaven, about God and about Jesus. She was blessed with a "matchless mother" and a father who had only to be seen praying "to know how the saints prayed." She was scarcely three years old when she longed for the "blessed bread" and soon after that she was engaged in "spiritual conferences" with her sister, Céline, four years her senior. After the death of her mother, her sister Pauline became her "little mother," and the first thing she used to ask Thérèse in the morning was if she had raised her heart to God. Then while dressing her, Pauline spoke to her of God, and then they knelt and prayed together.

From the dawn of her existence she was surrounded with love, first from her mother and father and sisters, and then when her mother died the "truly maternal" love of her father and the care and affection of Marie and Pauline. She did not appear to have a close relationship with another sister, Léonie, but Céline was her bosom companion. Love, then, was

33

central to her young life, so that it would have been easy for her to grasp the meaning of the term "God is love."

Heaven was the first word she was able to read. When she went fishing with her father she spent a good deal of the time in deep thought and she "could dream only of heaven." At school, when the other children were playing, she sought a quiet corner where she thought "about God, about life, about eternity."

When she came to make her first communion, she tells us that "for a long time now Jesus and poor little Thérèse looked at and understood each other," but now "it was no longer simply a look, it was a fusion. I felt that I was loved" (*Story*, p. 77). But the great break-through came when she rediscovered her strength of soul at Christmas 1886. After that, she tells us, "I felt charity enter my soul." The experience of seeing the blood flow from the wounded hand of Christ in a picture of our Lord on the cross awakened in her a thirst for souls and she satisfied his thirst by winning souls with the "divine dew" that flowed from his wounds.

To win souls, she knew that she would have to give herself totally to the Lord, and when Pauline explained to her the life of Carmel, she realized that "Carmel was the desert where God wanted me to hide myself." She had no doubt that it was God who inspired her vocation. When she was preparing to break the news to her father she prayed to the apostles to intercede for her with God so that she would use the right words, and she adds: "Shouldn't they help the timid child who was chosen by God to be the apostle of apostles through her prayers and sacrifices in Carmel?" (*Story*, p. 107).

The Fatherly Love of God

The flower about to tell her story rejoices at having to publish the totally gratuitous gifts of Jesus. She knows that nothing in herself was capable of attracting the divine glances, and his mercy alone brought about everything that is good in her. Seven years have passed by since the little flower took root in the garden of the Spouse of Virgins, and now *three** lilies bloom in her presence. A little farther off another lily expands under the eyes of Jesus. The two stems who brought these flowers into existence are now reunited for all eternity in the heavenly fatherland. There they have found once again the four lilies the earth had not seen develop. Oh! may Jesus deign not to allow a long time to pass on these strange shores for the flowers left in exile. May the lily-plant be soon complete in heaven!**

I have just summed up in a few words, dear Mother, what God did for me. Now I will go into detail about the years of my childhood. I realize that here where others would see nothing but a tedious recital, your motherly heart will find some facts that are charming. Besides, the memories I'm about to evoke are also yours since my childhood unfolded near you, and I have the good fortune to belong to parents without equal who surrounded us both with the same cares and the same tenderness. Oh! may they bless the littlest of their children and help her to sing the divine mercies!

In the story of my soul, up until my entrance into Carmel, I distinguish three separate periods. The first is not the least fruitful in memories in spite of its short duration. It extends from the dawn of my reason till our dear mother's departure for heaven.

God granted me the favor of opening my intelligence at an early age and of imprinting childhood recollections so deeply on my memory that it seems the things I'm about to recount happened only yesterday. Jesus in his love willed, perhaps, that I know the matchless mother he had given me, but whom his hand hastened to crown in heaven.

---

* In Thérèse's writings italics will indicate the points where she placed particular emphasis by underlining one or more times.

**Thérèse herself is the "little flower"; her sisters, Marie, Pauline and Céline are the "three lilies." The other "lily" referred to is Léonie who joined the Visitation Sisters in Caen. The "two stems" are the parents, Louis and Zélie Martin. The "four lilies" they found in heaven are their two sons and two daughters who died in infancy.

God was pleased all through my life to surround me with *love*, and the first memories I have are stamped with smiles and the most tender caresses. But although he placed so much *love* near me, he also sent much love into my little heart, making it warm and affectionate. I loved Mamma and Papa very much and showed my tenderness for them in a thousand ways, for I was very expressive.

On Sunday, as I was too little to go to the services, Mamma stayed with me; I was very good, walking around on tiptoe during the Mass; but as soon as I saw the door open, there was an explosion of joy! I would throw myself in front of my *pretty* little sister, *"adorned like a chapel,"** and say: "Oh! little Céline, hurry, give me the blessed bread!" Sometimes she didn't have it because she arrived too late. What to do? I wasn't able to be without it as this was *"my Mass."* A way was soon found. "You haven't any blessed bread? Then make some." No sooner said than done. Céline got a chair, opened the cupboard, took the bread, cut off a slice, and then very *gravely* recited a *Hail Mary* over it, and then she gave it to me. After asking a sign of the cross I would eat it with *great devotion,* finding it *tasted* the same as the *blessed bread.*

We carried on *spiritual conferences* together frequently. Here is a sample taken from one of Mamma's letters: "Our two little dears, Céline and Thérèse, are angels of benediction, little cherubs. Thérèse is the joy and happiness of Marie and even her glory; it's incredible how proud she is of her. It's true she has very rare answers for one her age; she surpasses Céline in this who is twice her age. Céline said the other day: 'How is it that God can be present in a small host?' The little one said: 'That is not surprising, God is all-powerful.' 'What does all-powerful mean?' 'It means he can do what he wants!' "

One day, Léonie, thinking she was too big to be playing any longer with dolls, came to us with a basket filled with dresses and pretty pieces for making others; her doll was resting on top. "Here, my little sisters, *choose;* I'm giving you all this." Céline stretched out her hand and took a little ball of wool which pleased her. After a moment's reflection, I stretched out mine saying: "I choose all!" and I took the basket without further ceremony. Those who witnessed the scene saw nothing wrong and even Céline herself didn't dream of complaining (besides, she had all

---

* "Adorned like a chapel" was an expression used by Louis Martin to describe how beautiful something was.

sorts of toys, her godfather gave her lots of presents, and Louise found ways of getting her everything she desired).

This little incident of my childhood is a summary of my whole life; later on when perfection was set before me, I understood that to become a *saint* one had to suffer much, seek out always the most perfect thing to do, and forget self. I understood, too, there were many degrees of perfection and each soul was free to respond to the advances of our Lord, to do little or much for him, in a word, to *choose* among the sacrifices he was asking. Then, as in the days of my childhood, I cried out: "My God *'I choose all!'* I don't want to be a *saint by halves,* I'm not afraid to suffer for you, I fear only one thing: to keep my *own will;* so take it, for *'I choose all'* that you will!"

(Story, I)

Finding Love in Hardship:
The Death of Her Mother

The day of Mamma's departure or the day after, Papa took me in his arms and said: "Come, kiss your poor little mother for the last time." Without a word I placed my lips on her forehead. I don't recall having cried very much, neither did I speak to anyone about the feelings I experienced. I looked and listened in silence. No one had any time to pay any attention to me, and I saw many things they would have hidden from me. For instance, once I was standing before the lid of the coffin which had been placed upright in the hall. I sopped for a long time gazing at it. Though I'd never seen one before, I understood what it was. I was so little that in spite of Mamma's small stature, I had to *raise* my head to take in its full height. It appeared *large* and *dismal.*

I must admit, Mother, my happy disposition completely changed after Mamma's death. I, once so full of life, became timid and retiring, sensitive to an excessive degree. One look was enough to reduce me to tears, and the only way I was content was to be left alone completely. I could not bear the company of strangers and found my joy only within the intimacy of the family.

And still I continued to be surrounded with the most delicate *tenderness.* Our father's *very affectionate heart* seemed to be enriched now with a truly maternal love! You and Marie, Mother, were you not *the most tender* and selfless of mothers? Ah! if God had not showered his beneficent *rays* upon his little flower, she could never have accustomed herself to earth, for she was too weak to stand up against the rains and the storms. She needed warmth, a gentle dew, and the springtime breezes. Never were these lacking. Jesus had her find them beneath the snow of trial!

I experienced no regret whatsoever at leaving Alençon; children are fond of change, and it was with pleasure that I came to Lisieux. I recall the trip, our arrival at Aunt's home; and I can still picture Jeanne and Marie waiting for us at the door. I was very fortunate in having such nice little cousins. I loved them very much, as also Aunt and especially Uncle; however, he frightened me, and I wasn't as much at ease in his home as I was at Les Buissonnets, for there my life was truly happy.

In the morning you used to come to me and ask me if I had raised my heart to God, and then you dressed me. While dressing me you spoke about him and afterwards we knelt down and said our prayers together. The reading lesson came later and the first word I was able to read without help was "heaven." My dear godmother took charge of the writing lessons and you, Mother, all the rest. I enjoyed no great facility in learning, but I did have a very good memory. Catechism and sacred history were my favorite subjects and these I studied with joy. Grammar frequently caused me to shed many tears. You no doubt recall the trouble I had with the masculine and feminine genders!

I recall during the walk on the seashore a man and a woman were looking at me as I ran ahead of Papa. They came and asked him if I were his little daughter and said I was a very pretty little girl. Papa said "Yes," but I noticed the sign he made to them not to pay me any compliments. . . . You always took great care, Mother, to allow me to come in contact with nothing that could destroy my innocence, and you saw to it, too, that I heard nothing capable of giving rise to vanity in my heart. As I listened to what you and Marie said, and as you had never directed any compliments to me, I gave no great importance to the words or admiring glances of this woman.

In the evening at that moment when the sun seems to bathe itself in the immensity of the waves, leaving a *luminous trail* behind, I went and sat down on a huge rock with *Pauline*. Then I recalled the touching story of the "Golden Trail." I contemplated this luminous trail for a long time. It was to me the image of God's grace shedding its light across the path the little white-sailed vessel had to travel. And near Pauline, I made the resolution never to wander far away from the glance of Jesus in order to travel peacefully toward the eternal shore! My life passed by tranquilly and happily. The affection with which I was surrounded at Les Buissonnets helped me grow. I was undoubtedly big enough now to commence the struggle, to commence knowing the world and the miseries with which it was filled.

(*Story*, II)

I was eight and a half when Léonie left boarding school and I replaced her at the Abbey.* I have often heard it said that the time spent at school is the best and happiest of one's life. It wasn't this way for me. The five years I spent in school were the saddest in my life, and if I hadn't had Céline with me, I couldn't have remained there and would have become sick in a month. The poor little flower had become accustomed to burying her fragile roots in *a chosen soil* made purposely for her. It seemed hard for her to see herself among flowers of all kinds with roots frequently indelicate; and she had to find in the *common soil* the food necessary for her sustenance!

You had instructed me so well, dear Mother, that when I went to boarding school I was the most advanced of the children of my age. I was placed, as a result, in a class where the pupils were all older than I. One of them was about thirteen or fourteen and she wasn't too intelligent, but she was really adept at influencing the students and even the teachers. When she noticed I was so young, almost always first in the class, and loved by all the Sisters, she experienced a jealousy pardonable in a student. She made me pay in a thousand ways for my little successes.

As I was timid and sensitive by nature, I didn't know how to defend myself and was content to cry without saying a word and without complaining *even to you* about what I was suffering. I didn't have enough virtue, however, to rise above these miseries of life, so my poor little heart suffered very much.

I have said nothing of my close relationship with Céline and if I had to recount everything I would never come to an end. At Lisieux the roles had changed, for Céline had become a naughty little rascal and Thérèse was no longer anything but a sweet little girl, much given to crying. This did not prevent Céline and Thérèse from loving each other more and more,

---

* "The Abbey"—a school run by the Benedictine Sisters for day-boarders.

but at times there were little arguments. These were not of a serious nature and basically they were both of the same mind. I can truly say that *never* did my little sister cause me any *trouble,* but was always a ray of sunshine for me, giving me much joy and consolation. Who can say with what intrepidity she defended me at the Abbey when I was accused of something? She took such good care of my health that I was wearied with her at times. What never wearied me, though, was *to see her at play.* She arranged our group of little dolls and conducted class like a truly clever teacher. She took care that her girls were always good, while mine were often put out of class because of bad behavior. She used to tell me all the new things she had just learned in class, which amused me very much; I looked upon her as a fountain of knowledge.

I had received the name: "Céline's little girl," and when she was irritated with me, her greatest sign of displeasure was to say: "You're no longer my little girl; that's over with, and I'll *always remember it!*" All I had to do was to start crying like a Magdalene, begging her to consider me still as her "little girl." Very soon she kissed me and promised me to *remember nothing.* To console me once she took one of her dolls and said; "My dear, embrace your Aunt!" The doll was in such a rush to embrace me tenderly that her two little arms went up *my nose.*

I have preserved a very sweet memory of the preparation you, my dear Mother, had Céline make. You took her, each evening, on your knees and spoke to her of the great action she was about to perform; I listened eagerly in order to prepare myself also, but very often you told me to go away as I was too little. Then my heart was very heavy and I thought four years was not too long to prepare to receive God.

One evening, I heard you say that from the time one received one's first communion, one had to commence living a new life, and I immediately made the resolution not to wait for that day but to commence the very same time as Céline. Never had I felt I loved her as much as I did during her three-day retreat; for the first time in my life, I was separated from her and I didn't sleep in her bed. The first day, forgetting she was not going to return, I kept a small bunch of cherries which Papa had brought me in order to eat them with her. When I didn't see her returning home, I was really sad. Papa consoled me by saying he would take me the next day to the Abbey to see my Céline and that I would give her another bunch of cherries! The day of Céline's first communion left me with an impression similar to my own first communion. When awakening in the morning all alone in the big bed, I felt *inundated with joy.* "It's today! The great day has arrived." I repeated this over and over again. It seemed it was I who was going to make my first communion. I believe I received great graces that day and I consider it one of the most beautiful in my life.

(Story, III)

Discovering Love in the Eucharist

The "beautiful day of days" finally arrived. The *smallest details* of that heavenly day have left unspeakable memories in my soul! The joyous awakening at dawn, the *respectful* embraces of the teachers and our older companions! The large room filled with *snow-white dresses* in which each child was to be clothed in her turn! Above all, the procession into the chapel and the singing of the *morning* hymn: "O altar of God, where the angels are hovering!"

I don't want to enter into detail here. There are certain things that lose their perfume as soon as they are exposed to the air; there are deep *spiritual thoughts* which cannot be expressed in human language without losing their intimate and heavenly meaning; they are similar to ". . . *the white stone I will give to him who conquers, with a name written on the stone which no one knows except him who receives it*" (Rv 2:17).

Ah! how sweet was that first kiss of Jesus! It was a kiss of *love*; I felt that I *was loved,* and I said: "I love you, and I give myself to you forever!" There were no demands made, no struggles, no sacrifices; for a long time now Jesus and poor little Thérèse *looked at* and understood each other. That day, it was no longer simply a *look,* it was a fusion; they were no longer two, Thérèse had vanished as a drop of water is lost in the immensity of the ocean. Jesus alone remained; he was the master, the king. Had not Thérèse asked him to take away her *liberty,* for her *liberty* frightened her? She felt so feeble and fragile that she wanted to be united forever to the divine Strength! Her joy was too great, too deep for her to contain, and tears of consolation soon flowed, to the great consternation of her companions. They asked one another: "Why was she crying? Was there something bothering her?" — "No, it was because her mother was

not there or her sister whom she loves so much, her sister the Carmelite. "
They did not understand that all the joy of heaven having entered my
heart, this exiled heart was unable to bear it without shedding tears. Oh!
no, the absence of Mamma didn't cause me any sorrow on the day of my
first communion. Wasn't heaven itself in my soul, and hadn't Mamma
taken her place there a long time ago? Thus in receiving Jesus' visit, I
received also Mamma's. She blessed me and rejoiced at my happiness. I
was not crying because of Pauline's absence. I would have been happy
to see her by my side, but for a long time I had accepted my sacrifice of
her. On that day, joy alone filled my heart and I united myself to her who
gave herself irrevocably to him who gave himself so lovingly to me!

(Story, IV)

The Grace-Filled Christmas of 1886

Although God showered his graces upon me, it wasn't because I
merited them because I was still very imperfect. I had a great desire, it is
true, to practice virtue, but I went about it in a strange way. Being the
youngest in the family, I wasn't accustomed to doing things for myself.
Céline tidied up the room in which we slept, and I myself didn't do any
housework whatsoever. After Marie's entrance into Carmel, it sometimes
happened that I tried to make up the bed to please God, or else in the
evening, when Céline was away, I'd bring in her plants. But as I already
said, it was for *God alone* I was doing these things and should not have
expected any *thanks* from creatures. Alas, it was just the opposite. If
Céline was unfortunate enough not to seem happy or surprised because
of these little services, I became unhappy and proved it by my tears.

I was really unbearable because of my extreme touchiness; if I happened to cause anyone I loved some little trouble, even unwittingly,
instead of forgetting about it and not *crying,* which made matters worse,
I *cried* like a Magdalene and then when I began to cheer up, I'd begin to
cry again for having cried. All arguments were useless; I was quite unable
to correct this terrible fault. I really don't know how I could entertain the
thought of entering Carmel when I was still in the *swaddling clothes of a
child!*

God would have to work a little miracle to make me *grow up* in an instant, and this miracle he performed on that unforgettable Christmas day. On that luminous *night* which sheds such light on the delights of the Holy Trinity, Jesus, the gentle, *little* Child of only one hour, changed the night of my soul into rays of light. On that *night* when he made himself subject to *weakness* and suffering for love of me, he made me *strong* and courageous, arming me with his weapons. Since that night I have never been defeated in any combat, but rather walked from victory to victory, beginning, so to speak, *"to run as a giant"* (Ps 18:6)! The source of my tears was dried up and has since re-opened rarely and with great difficulty. This justified what was often said to me: "You cry so much during your childhood, you'll no longer have tears to shed later on!"

It was December 25, 1886, that I received the grace of leaving my childhood, in a word, the grace of my complete conversion. We had come back from Midnight Mass where I had the happiness of receiving the *strong* and *powerful* God. Upon arriving at Les Buissonnets, I used to love to take my shoes from the chimney-corner and examine the presents in them; this old custom had given us so much joy in our youth that Céline wanted to continue treating me as a baby since I was the youngest in the family. Papa had always loved to see my happiness and listen to my cries of delight as I drew each surprise from the *magic shoes,* and my dear king's gaiety increased my own happiness very much. However, Jesus desired to show me that I was to give up the defects of my childhood and so he withdrew its innocent pleasures. He permitted Papa, tired out after the Midnight Mass, to experience annoyance when seeing my shoes at the fireplace, and that he speak those words which pierced my heart: "Well, fortunately, this will be the last year!" I was going upstairs, at the time, to remove my hat, and Céline, knowing how sensitive I was and seeing the tears already glistening in my eyes, wanted to cry too, for she loved me very much and understood my grief. She said "Oh, Thérèse, don't go downstairs; it would cause you too much grief to look at your slippers right now!" But Thérèse was no longer the same; Jesus had changed her heart! Forcing back my tears, I descended the stairs rapidly; controlling the pounding of my heart, I took my slippers and placed them in front of Papa, and withdrew all the objects joyfully. I had the happy appearance of a queen. Having regained his own cheerfulness, Papa was laughing; Céline believed it was all a *dream!* Fortunately, it was a sweet reality; Thérèse had discovered once again the strength of soul which she had lost at the age of four and a half, and she was to preserve it forever!

On that *night of light* began the third period of my life, the most beautiful and the most filled with graces from heaven. The work I had been unable to do in ten years was done by Jesus in one instant, contenting himself with my *good will* which was never lacking. I could say to him like his apostles: "Master, I fished all night and caught nothing" (Lk 5:5). More merciful to me than he was to his disciples, Jesus *took the net himself,* cast it, and drew it in filled with fish. He made me a fisher of *souls.* I experienced a great desire to work for the conversion of sinners, a desire I hadn't felt so intensely before.

I felt *charity* enter into my soul, and the need to forget myself and to please others; since then I've been happy! One Sunday, looking at a picture of our Lord on the cross, I was struck by the blood flowing from one of the divine hands. I felt a great pang of sorrow when thinking this blood was falling to the ground without anyone's hastening to gather it up. I was resolved to remain in spirit at the foot of the cross and to receive the divine dew. I understood I was then to pour it out upon souls. The cry of Jesus on the cross sounded continually in my heart: *"I thirst!"* (Jn 19:28). These words ignited within me an unknown and very living fire. I wanted to give my Beloved to drink and I felt myself consumed with a *thirst for souls.* As yet, it was not the souls of priests that attracted me, but those of *great sinners;* I *burned* with the desire to snatch them from the eternal flames.

To awaken my zeal God showed me my desires were pleasing to him. I heard talk of a great criminal just condemned to death for some horrible crimes; everything pointed to the fact that he would die impenitent. I wanted at all costs to prevent him from falling into hell, and to attain my purpose I employed every means imaginable. Feeling that of myself I could do nothing, I offered to God all the infinite merits of our Lord, the treasures of the Church, and finally I begged Céline to have a Mass offered for my intentions. I didn't dare ask this myself for fear of being obliged to say it was for Pranzini, the great criminal. I didn't even want to tell Céline, but she asked me such tender and pressing questions, I confided my secret to her. Far from laughing at me, she asked if she could help convert *my sinner.* I accepted gratefully, for I would have wished all creatures would unite with me to beg grace for the guilty man.

I felt in the depths of my heart *certain* that our desires would be granted, but to obtain courage to pray for sinners I told God I was sure he would pardon the poor, unfortunate Pranzini; that I'd believe this even if he went to his death without *any signs* of *repentance* or without *having gone to confession.* I was absolutely confident in the mercy of Jesus. But I was begging him for a *"sign"* of repentance only for my own simple consolation.

My prayer was answered to the letter! In spite of Papa's prohibition that we read no papers, I didn't think I was disobeying when reading the passages pertaining to Pranzini. The day after his execution I found the newspaper *"La Croix."* I opened it quickly and what did I see? Ah! my tears betrayed my emotion and I was obliged to hide. Pranzini had not gone to confession. He had mounted the scaffold and was preparing to place his head in the formidable opening, when suddenly, seized by an inspiration, he turned, took hold of the *crucifix* the priest was holding out to him and *kissed* the *sacred wounds three times!* Then his soul went to receive the *merciful* sentence of him who declares that in heaven there will be more joy over one sinner who does penance than over ninety-nine just who have no need of repentance (Lk 15:7).

I had obtained the "sign" I requested, and this sign was a perfect replica of the grace Jesus had given me when he attracted me to pray for sinners. Wasn't it before the *wounds of Jesus,* when seeing his divine *blood* flowing, that thirst for souls had entered my heart? I wished to give them this *immaculate blood* to drink, this blood which was to purify them from their stains, and the lips of my *"first child"* were pressed to the sacred wounds!

What an unspeakably sweet response! After this unique grace my desire to save souls grew each day, and I seemed to hear Jesus say to me what he said to the Samaritan woman: *"Give me to drink!"* (Jn 4:7). It was a true interchange of love: to souls I was giving the blood of Jesus, to Jesus I was offering these same souls refreshed by the divine dew. I slaked his thirst and the more I gave him to drink, the more the thirst of my poor little soul increased, and it was this ardent thirst he was giving me as the most delightful drink of his love.

(Story, V)

Love and Trust:
The Fight for Her Vocation

After receiving Papa's permission, I believed I'd be able to fly to Carmel without any fears, but painful trials were still to prove my vocation. It was with trembling I confided my resolution to Uncle. He showed me great tenderness but did not grant me his permission to leave. He forbade me to speak about my vocation to him until I was seventeen. It was contrary to human prudence, he said, to have a child of fifteen enter Carmel. This Carmelite life was, in the eyes of many, a life of mature reflection, and it would be doing a great wrong to the religious life to allow an inexperienced child to embrace it. Everybody would be talking about it, etc., etc. He even said that for him to decide to allow me to leave would require a miracle. I saw all reasoning with him was useless and so I left, my heart plunged into the most profound bitterness. My only consolation was prayer. I begged Jesus to perform the miracle demanded, since at this price only I'd be able to answer his call.

A long time passed by before I dared speak to him again. It was very difficult for me to go to his home, and he himself seemed to be no longer considering my vocation. I learned later on that my great sadness influenced him very much. Before allowing any ray of hope to shine in my soul, God willed to send me a painful martyrdom lasting three days. Oh! never had I understood so well as during this trial, the sorrow of Mary and Joseph during their three-day search for the divine Child Jesus. I was in a sad desert, or rather my soul was like a fragile boat delivered up to the mercy of the waves and having no pilot. I knew Jesus was there sleeping in my boat, but the night was so black it was impossible to see him; nothing gave me any light, not a single flash came to break the dark clouds. No doubt, lightning is a dismal light, but at least if the storm had broken out in earnest I would have been able to see Jesus for one passing moment. But it was night! The dark night of the soul! I felt I was all alone in the garden of Gethsemane like Jesus, and I found no consolation on earth or from heaven; God himself seemed to have abandoned me. Nature seemed to share in my bitter sadness, for during these three days the sun did not shine and the rain poured down in torrents. (I have noticed in all the serious circumstances of my life that nature always reflected the image of my soul. On days filled with tears the heavens cried along with me; on days of joy the sun sent forth its joyful rays in profusion and the blue skies were not obscured by a single cloud.)

Finally, on the fourth day which happened to be a Saturday, the day consecrated to the sweet Queen of heaven, I went to see Uncle. What was my surprise when I saw him looking at me, and, without expressing any desire to speak to him, he had me come into his study! He began by making some gentle reproaches because I appeared to be afraid of him, and then he said it wasn't necessary to beg for a miracle, that he had only asked God to give him "a simple change of heart" and that he had been answered. Ah! I was not tempted to beg for a miracle because the miracle had been granted; Uncle was not longer the same. Without making any allusion whatsoever to "human prudence," he told me I was a little flower God wanted to gather, and he would no longer oppose it! This definitive response was truly worthy of him. For the third time now, this Christian of another age allowed one of the adopted daughters of his heart to go bury herself far from the world. Aunt, too, was admirable in her tenderness and prudence. I don't remember her saying a single word during my trial that could have increased my sufferings. I understood she pitied her little Thérèse. But when Uncle gave his consent, she too gave hers, but at the same time she showed me in a thousand little ways the great sorrow my departure would be for her. Alas, our dear relatives were far from expecting the same sacrifice would be asked of them twice over. But when God stretches out his hand to ask, his hand is never *empty,* and his intimate friends can draw from him the courage and strength they need.

My heart is carrying me far from my subject and so, regretfully, I return to it. You can easily understand, dear Mother, how, after Uncle's response, I took the road back to Les Buissonnets with happiness flooding my heart. It was under "a *beautiful* sky, from which all the clouds were dispersed"! In my soul, too, the night had come to an end. Awakening, Jesus brought back joy, the noise of the waves was abated, and in place of the wind of trial, a light breeze expanded my sail and I believed I'd reach the blessed *shore,* now seemingly so close! It was really very close to my boat, but *more than one storm* was still to arise. Hiding from me the view of the luminous beacon, these storms caused me to fear lest I should be driven far from the shore so ardently desired without any hope of return.

I obtained, then, Uncle's permission and a few days afterwards went to see you, dear Mother. I told you of my joy at seeing that my trials were all over. What was my surprise and sadness when you told me that the superior was not giving his consent to my entrance until I was twenty-one. No one had thought of this opposition, and it was the most insurmountable of all. Without giving up hope, however, I went myself with Papa and Céline to pay him a visit, trying to change his mind by showing I really had a Carmelite vocation.

He received us coldly; my *incomparable* little father joined his insistence to mine but in vain. Nothing would change the superior's attitude. He told me there wasn't any danger in staying at home, I could lead a Carmelite life there, and if I didn't take the discipline all was not lost, etc., etc. He ended by saying he was only the *bishop's delegate*, and if the latter wished me to enter Carmel, he himself would have nothing to say.

I left the rectory in *tears*, and fortunately my umbrella was able to hide them as the *rain* was coming down in torrents. Papa was at a loss as to how to console me. He promised to accompany me to Bayeux the moment I expressed my desire to go there since I was determined *to do all within my power*, even saying I would go to the *Holy Father* if the bishop did not want to allow me to enter at fifteen.

(*Story*, V)

PERIOD TWO

Her Response to Love—The Early Years in Carmel

1888-1890

"I was to pass through many trials, but the divine call was so strong that had I been forced to pass through flames, I would have done it out of love for Jesus" (*Story*, p. 106). Once Thérèse was convinced that she was called to save souls and that the place to do so was Carmel, she left no stone unturned to achieve her goal, even though she was not yet fifteen. At last, all obstacles were removed and the day of her entry was fixed for April 9, 1888.

Only one who has passed through the trauma of severing one's links with one's family can appreciate what Thérèse felt as she bade farewell to her family, especially her father. But she took Christ at his word, that when his call comes one must be prepared to leave all for his sake.

Thérèse entered Carmel to save souls and to pray for priests, and Jesus gave her to understand that this would be achieved through suffering, not suffering for its own sake but as a proof of love, just as he himself had shown his love for humankind by his bitter passion and death. Thérèse wanted to hide herself with him, contemplating that divine face which was "hidden" during his life-giving sufferings.

Her sufferings were caused by persons such as the prioress, a companion novice and the novice mistress, often without their being aware of the fact; from the circumstances of the life, the food, the cold; from not being able to relate to her own sisters as she did when they were at home, because it was for love of Jesus and not for love of her sisters that she came to Carmel.

Above all, her sufferings came from aridity in prayer and from the illness of her father. We see in her letters to Céline how deeply she was affected by the humiliation of her father, but far from complaining she thanked God for giving them this opportunity of accumulating merit, thus winning souls and gaining heaven. At this time she consoles Céline with the thought of heaven and the joys awaiting them there. She had not yet reached the stage where she was detached from the thought of meriting. Later she would leave everything in the hands of Jesus and let him be her "banker."

In the meantime, she used the means at her disposal for showing her love for Jesus, mere nothings but done with love. Poverty had a particular attraction for her and she assiduously practiced the only mortification allowed her, that of mortifying her self-love, which she says did her more good than corporal penances.

All of this was a preparation for the definite gift of herself to Jesus. At last the "beautiful day of my wedding arrived" (*Story*, p. 166). "I offered myself to Jesus in order to accomplish his will perfectly in me without creatures ever being able to place any obstacle in the way" (*Story*, p. 167).

Love's Request: More Thorns than Roses

The day chosen for my entrance into Carmel was April 9, 1888, the same day the community was celebrating the feast of the Annunciation, transferred because of Lent. The evening before, the whole family gathered round the table where I was to sit for the last time. Ah! how heartrending these family reunions can really be! When you would like to see yourself forgotten, the most tender caresses and words are showered upon you making the sacrifice of separation felt all the more.

Papa was not saying very much, but his gaze was fixed upon me lovingly. Aunt cried from time to time and Uncle paid me many affectionate compliments. Jeanne and Marie gave me all sorts of little attentions, especially Marie, who, taking me aside, asked pardon for the troubles she thought she caused me. My dear little Léonie, who had returned from the Visitation a few months previously, kissed and embraced me often. There is only Céline, about whom I have not spoken, but you can well imagine, dear Mother, how we spent that last night together.

On the morning of the great day, casting a last look upon Les Buissonnets, that beautiful cradle of my childhood which I was never to see again, I left on my dear king's arm to climb Mount Carmel. As on the evening before, the whole family was reunited to hear Holy Mass and receive communion. As soon as Jesus descended into the hearts of my relatives, I heard nothing around me but sobs. I was the only one who didn't shed any tears, but my heart was beating *so violently* it seemed impossible to walk when they signaled for me to come to the enclosure door. I advanced, however, asking myself whether I was going to die because of the beating of my heart! Ah! what a moment that was! One would have to experience it to know what it is.

My emotion was not noticed exteriorly. After embracing all the members of the family, I knelt down before my matchless father for his blessing, and to give it to me he placed *himself on his knees* and blessed me, tears flowing down his cheeks. It was a spectacle to make the angels smile, this spectacle of an old man presenting his child, still in the springtime of life, to the Lord! A few moments later, the doors of the holy ark closed upon me, and there I was received by the *dear Sisters* who embraced me. They had acted as mothers to me and I was going to take them as models for my actions from now on. My desires were at last accomplished; my soul experienced a *peace* so sweet, so deep, it would be impossible to express it. For seven years and a half that inner peace has remained my lot, and has not abandoned me in the midst of the greatest trials.

I was led, as are all postulants, to the choir immediately after my entrance into the cloister. The choir was in darkness because the Blessed Sacrament was exposed and what struck me first were the eyes of our holy Mother Geneviève which were fixed on me. I remained kneeling for a moment at her feet, thanking God for the grace he gave me of knowing a saint, and then I followed Mother Marie de Gonzague into the different places of the community. Everything thrilled me; I felt as though I was transported into a desert; our little cell, above all, filled me with joy. But the joy I was experiencing was *calm,* the lightest breeze did not undulate the quiet waters upon which my little boat was floating and no cloud darkened my blue heaven. Ah! I was fully recompensed for all my trials. With what deep joy I repeated those words: "I am here forever and ever!"

This happiness was not passing. It didn't take its flight with "the illusions of the first days." *Illusions,* God gave me the grace *not to have a single one* when entering Carmel. I found the religious life to be *exactly* as I had imagined it, no sacrifice astonished me and yet, as you know, dear Mother, my first steps met with more thorns than roses! Yes, suffering opened wide its arms to me and I threw myself into them with love. I had declared at the feet of Jesus-Victim, in the examination preceding my profession, what I had come to Carmel for: "I came to save souls and especially to pray for priests." When one wishes to attain a goal, one must use the means; Jesus made me understand that it was through suffering that he wanted to give me souls, and my attraction for suffering grew in proportion to its increase. This was my way for five years; exteriorly nothing revealed my suffering which was all the more painful since I alone was aware of it.

(*Story*, VII)

Love's Demand:
Detachment of All Things Created

I had already received, since my taking of the habit, abundant lights on religious perfection, principally with regard to the vow of poverty.

During my postulancy, I was content to have nice things for my use and to have everything necessary for me at my disposal. "*My Director*"* bore this patiently, for he doesn't like pointing everything out at once to souls. He generally gives his light little by little. At the beginning of my spiritual life when I was thirteen or fourteen, I used to ask myself what I would have to strive for later on because I believed it was quite impossible for me to understand perfection better. I learned very quickly since then that the more one advances, the more one sees the goal is still far off. And now I am simply resigned to see myself always imperfect and in this I find my joy.

But let us return to the lessons "*My Director*" gave me. One evening, after Compline, I was looking in vain for our lamp on the shelves reserved for this purpose. It was during the time of the Great Silence and so it was impossible to complain to anyone about my loss. I understood that a Sister, believing she was taking her lamp, picked up ours which I really needed. Instead of feeling annoyed at being thus deprived of it, I was really happy, feeling that poverty consists in being deprived not only of agreeable things but of indispensable things too. And so in this *exterior darkness,* I was interiorly illumined!

I was taken up, at this time, with a real attraction for objects that were both very ugly and the least convenient. So it was with joy that I saw myself deprived of a pretty *little jug* in our cell and supplied with another large one, *all chipped.* I was exerting much effort, too, at not excusing myself, which was very difficult for me, especially with our novice mistress from whom I didn't want to hide anything. Here was my first victory, not too great but it cost me a whole lot. A little vase set behind a window was broken, and our mistress, thinking it was my fault, showed it to me and told me to be more careful in the future. Without a word, I kissed the floor, promising to be more careful in the future. Because of my lack of virtue these little practices cost me very much and I had to console myself with the thought that at the last judgment everything would be revealed. I noticed this: when one performs her duty, never excusing herself, no one knows it; on the contrary, imperfections appear immediately.

I applied myself to practicing little virtues, not having the capability

---

* It was Fr. Pichon, the spiritual director of Marie, who said to Thérèse: "My child, may our Lord always be your superior and novice master." Thérèse tells us that he was so in fact, and also her "Director" (cf. *Story,* p. 150).

of practicing the great. For instance, I loved to fold up the mantles forgotten by the Sisters, and to render them all sorts of little services. Love for mortification was given me, and this love was all the greater because I was allowed nothing by way of satisfying it. The only little mortification I was doing while still in the world, which consisted in not leaning my back against any support while seated, was forbidden me because of my inclination to stoop. Alas! my ardor for penances would not have lasted long had the superiors allowed them. The penances they did allow me consisted in mortifying my self-love, which did me much more good than corporal penances.

(Story, VII)

J. M. J. T.

Monday, July 23, 1888

Jesus alone †

Darling Sister,

Your Thérèse understood your whole soul; she read still more deeply into it than you wrote about it. I understood the sadness of Sunday; I experienced it all. . . . It seemed to me when I was reading it that the same soul animates us. There is something so sensitive between our souls that makes them so much alike. We have always been together, our joys, our pains, everything has been in common. Ah! I feel that this is continuing in Carmel; never, no, never shall we be separated. You know that it is only the yellow lily* that could separate us a little. I tell you this because I am sure that the white lily will always be your lot since you have chosen him and he has chosen you first. . . . Do you understand the lilies. . . .

I was sometimes wondering why Jesus had taken me first; now I have understood. . . . You know that your soul is a lily *immortelle*. Jesus can do all he wills with it. It matters little whether it be in one place or another; it will always be *immortelle*. The tempest cannot make the yellow of its stamen fall on its white-scented calyx; it is Jesus who made it that way. He is free, and so one is to ask him why he gives his graces to one soul rather than another. At the side of this lily, Jesus has placed another, its faithful companion. They grew up together but one was *immortelle*, and

---

* "Yellow lily" in the common language of the Carmel meant marriage.

the other was not. It was necessary that Jesus take his lily before its flower opened so that the two lilies be for him. . . . One was weak, the other was strong; Jesus took the weak one, and he left the other so as to embellish it with a new splendor. . . . Jesus asks *all* from his two lilies; he wills to leave them nothing but their white dress. *All!* Has *immortelle* understood her little sister? . . .

Life is burdensome. What bitterness . . . but what sweetness. Yes, life is painful for us. It is hard to begin a day of work. The feeble bud has seen it just as the beautiful lily has. If we feel Jesus present, oh! then we would really do all for him, but no, he seems a thousand leagues away. We are all alone with ourselves. Oh! what annoying company when Jesus is not there. But what is this sweet Friend doing then? Doesn't he see our anguish, the weight that is oppressing us? Where is he? Why doesn't he come to console us since we have him alone for a friend? Alas, he is not far; he is there, very close. He is looking at us, and he *is begging* this sorrow, this agony from us. He needs it for souls and for our soul. He wants to give us such a beautiful recompense, and his ambitions for us are very great. But how can he say: "My turn," if ours hasn't come, if we have given him nothing? Alas, it does pain him to give us sorrows to drink, but he knows this is the only means of preparing us to "know him as *he knows himself* and to become *Gods ourselves*" (see 1 Cor 13:12). Oh! what a destiny. How great is our soul. . . .

Let us raise ourselves above what is passing away. Let us keep ourselves a distance from the earth. Higher up the air is pure. Jesus is hiding himself, but we can see him. When shedding tears, we are drying his, and the Blessed Virgin smiles. Poor Mother, she had so many sorrows because of us, and it is only right that we console her a little when we weep and suffer with her. . . .

I read this morning a passage of the gospel where it says: "I have not come to bring peace but the sword" (Mt 10:34). There remains nothing else for us to do but to fight, and when we don't have the strength, it is then that Jesus fights for us. . . . Together let us lay the axe to the root of the tree. . . .

Poor muddle-headed Thérèse. What a letter, what turmoil. . . . Oh! if I could only have said what I am thinking, Céline would have very much to read. . . .

Jesus is good to have allowed us to meet a mother like the one we have. What a treasure. Little sister, if you had seen her this morning at six o'clock, bringing me your letter. I was really moved. . . .

Jesus is asking *all, all, all*. As much as he can ask from the greatest Saints.

Your poor little sister,
Thérèse of the Child Jesus
p.c.ind.

(L 57, to Céline)

J. M. J. T.

March 5, 1889

Jesus †

My dear Céline,

I cannot tell you how much good your dear little letter did me! . . . Now you are truly the *lily-immortelle* of Jesus. Oh! how pleased he is with his lily, how lovingly he looks on his dear flower, who wants *him alone*, who has no other desire except that of consoling him. . . .

Each new suffering, each new agony of her heart is like a light breeze which will carry to Jesus the perfume of his lily; then he will smile lovingly, and he will immediately prepare a new sorrow. He is filling the chalice to the brim, thinking that the more his lily grows in love the more, too, must it grow in suffering! . . .

What a privilege Jesus grants us in sending such a great *sorrow*. Ah! *eternity* will not be too long to thank him. He is giving us his favors just as he gave them to the greatest saints. Why this great predilection? . . . It is a secret which Jesus will reveal in our homeland on the day when "he will dry all the tears from our eyes" (Rv 21:4). . . . It is necessary that it be to *my soul* that I am speaking in this way, for otherwise I would not be understood, but it is to her that I am addressing myself, and all my thoughts were anticipated by her. However, what she does not know perhaps is the love that Jesus has for her, a love that demands *all*. There is nothing that is impossible for him. He does not want to set any limit to his lily's *sanctity;* his limit is that there is no limit! . . . Why should there be any? We are greater than the whole universe, and one day we *ourselves* shall have a divine existence. . . .

Oh! I thank Jesus for having placed a lily near our dear father, a lily that fears nothing, a lily that wishes rather *to die* than to abandon the *glorious* field in which the love of Jesus has placed it! . . .

Now we have no longer anything to hope for on earth, no longer anything but suffering and again suffering. When we have finished, suffering will still be there, extending its arms to us. Oh! what a lot worthy of envy. . . . The Cherubim in heaven envy our joy.

It was not for this that I was writing to my Céline, but it was to tell her to write to Mademoiselle Pauline about the misfortune that has struck us in Papa's illness. Laugh in your turn at your poor Thérèse, who approaches her subject at the end of her letter. Poor Léonie, I love her also; she is more unfortunate than we are, for Jesus has given her less. But *much* will be demanded from those to whom much has been given (see Lk 12:48).

Your little sister,

> Thérèse of the Child Jesus
> post.carm.ind.
>
> (L 83, to Céline)

J. M. J. T.

Carmel, March 12, 1889

(Long live Jesus! . . . How good it is to vow oneself to him, and to sacrifice oneself for his love). . . .

Céline! . . . This dear name echoes sweetly at the bottom of my heart! . . . Don't our hearts answer each other perfectly? . . .

I have a need this evening to come with my Céline in order to plunge myself into infinity. . . . I have to forget this earth. . . . Here below, everything tires me, everything is a burden to me. . . . I find only one joy, that of suffering for Jesus, but this *unfelt* joy is above every other joy! . . .

Life is passing away. . . . Eternity is advancing in great strides. . . . Soon we shall live the very life of Jesus. . . . After having drunk at the fountain of all sorrows, we shall be deified at the very fountain of all joys, all delights. . . . Soon, little sister, with one look, we shall be able to understand what is taking place within the inner depths of our being! . . .

The image of this world *is passing away* (1 Cor 7:31). . . . Soon we shall see new heavens, and a more radiant Sun will light up with its splendors ethereal oceans and infinite horizons! . . . Immensity will be our domain. . . . We shall no longer be prisoners on this earth of exile. . . . All will have *passed away*! . . . With our heavenly Spouse, we shall sail on lakes without any shores. . . . Infinity has no limits, no bottom, no shore! . . . (Courage, Jesus can hear the very last echo of our sorrow.) Our harps, at this moment, are hung on the willow which border the river of Babylon (see Ps 136:1-2). . . . But on the day of our deliverance, what songs will be heard . . . with what joy shall we make the strings of our instruments vibrate! . . .

Jesus' love for Céline can be understood only by Jesus! . . . Jesus has done foolish things for Céline. . . . Let Céline do *foolish things* for Jesus. . . . Love is repaid by love alone, and the *wounds* of love are healed only by love.

Let us really offer our sufferings to Jesus to save souls, poor souls! . . . They have less grace than we have, and still all the blood of a God was shed to save them. . . . And yet Jesus wills to make their salvation depend on one sigh from our heart. . . . What a mystery! If one sigh can save *a soul,* what can sufferings like ours not do? . . . Let us refuse Jesus nothing! . . .

The bell is ringing and I haven't yet written to poor Léonie. Give her my suggestions, kiss her, and tell her that I love her! . . . Let her be *very faithful* to grace, and Jesus will bless her. Let her ask Jesus what I want to say to her. I entrust him with my messages! . . .

See you soon! . . . Oh, heaven, heaven. When shall we be there?

Jesus' little *grain of Sand*

(L 85, to Céline)

The Love in Christ's Blood-Stained Face

J. M. J. T.

Carmel, April 4, 1889

Jesus †. . .

Dear little Céline,

Your letter gave great sadness to my soul! Poor little Papa! . . . No, the thoughts of Jesus are not our thoughts, and his ways are not our ways (see Is 55:8). . . .

He is offering us a chalice as bitter as our feeble nature can bear! . . .

Let us not withdraw our lips from this chalice prepared by the hand of Jesus. . . .
Let us see life as it really is. . . . It is a moment between two *eternities.*
. . . Let us suffer in *peace!* . . .
I admit that this word peace seemed a little strong to me, but the other day, when reflecting on it, I found the secret of suffering in peace. . . . The one who says *peace* is not saying joy, or at least, *felt* joy. . . . To suffer in peace it is enough to will all that Jesus wills. . . . To be the spouse of Jesus we *must* resemble Jesus, and Jesus is all bloody, he is crowned with thorns! . . .
"A thousand years in your eyes, Lord, are as yesterday, which has *passed*" (Ps 89:4)! . . .
"On the banks of the river of Babylon, we sat and wept when we remembered Sion. . . . We hung our harps on the willows in the fields. . . . Those who led us into captivity said to us: 'Sing for us one of the pleasant songs from Sion.' How could we sing the song of the Lord in a foreign land!" . . . Psalm of David (137:1-4). . . .
No, let us not sing the canticles of heaven to creatures. . . . But, like Cecilia, let us sing a melodious canticle in our heart to our Beloved! . . .
The canticle of suffering united to his sufferings is what delights his heart the most! . . .
Jesus is on fire with love for us . . . look at his adorable face! . . . Look at his eyes lifeless and lowered! Look at his wounds. . . . Look at Jesus in his face. . . . There you will see how he loves us.

Sister Thérèse
of the Child Jesus
of the Holy Face
nov.carm.ind.

(L 87, to Céline)

J. M. J. T.

Carmel, April 26, 1889

Jesus †! . . .

Jesus himself is taking charge of saying *happy birthday* for his fiancée's twenty years! . . .
What a twentieth year fruitful in *sufferings,* in choice graces! Twenty

years! an age filled with *illusion* . . . tell me what illusion are you leaving in the heart of my Céline? . . .

What memories between us! . . . It's a world of memories. . . . Yes, Jesus has his preferences; there are, in his garden, fruits which the sun of his love ripens almost in the twinkling of an eye. . . . Why are we of this number? . . . A question filled with mystery. . . . What reason can Jesus give us? Alas! his reason is that he has no reason! . . . Céline! Let us make use of Jesus' preference which has taught us so many things in so few years, and let us neglect nothing that can please him! . . . Ah! let us be adorned by the Sun of his *love*! . . . this sun is burning . . . let us be consumed by *love*! . . . St. Francis de Sales says: "When the fire of love is in a heart, all the furniture flies out the windows." Oh! let us allow nothing . . . nothing in our heart except Jesus! . . .

Let us not believe we can love without suffering, without suffering much. . . . Our *poor* nature is there! and it isn't there for nothing! . . . Our nature is our riches, our means of earning our bread! . . . It is so precious that Jesus came on earth purposely to take possession of it.

Let us suffer the bitter pain, without courage! . . . (Jesus suffered in *sadness*! Without sadness would the soul suffer! . . .) And still we would like to suffer generously, grandly! . . . Céline! what an illusion! . . . We'd never want to fall? . . . What does it matter, my Jesus, if I fall at each moment; *I see* my weakness through this and this is a great gain for me. . . . *You can see* through this what I can do and now you will be more tempted to carry me in your arms. . . . If you do not do it, it is because this pleases you to see me *on the ground*. . . . Then I am not going to be disturbed, but I shall always stretch out my arms suppliant and filled with love! . . . I cannot believe that you would abandon me! . . .

(It was *when* the saints were at the feet of our Lord that they encountered their crosses! . . .)

Dear Céline, sweet echo of my soul! . . . If you only knew my misery! . . . Oh! if you only knew. . . . Sanctity does not consist in saying beautiful things, it does not even consist in thinking them, in feeling them! . . . It consists in *suffering* and suffering *everything*. (Sanctity! We must conquer it at the point of the sword; we must *suffer* . . . we *must agonize*!). . .

A day will come when the shadows will disappear, and then there will remain only joy, inebriation. . . .

Let us profit from our one moment of suffering! . . . Let us see only each moment! . . . A moment is a treasure . . . one act of love will make us know Jesus better . . . it will bring us closer to him during the whole of *eternity!* . . .

Sister Thérèse
of the Child Jesus
of the Holy Face
nov.carm.ind.

(L 89, to Céline)

J. M. J. T.

Carmel, July 14, 1889

Jesus †

My dear Céline,
My soul doesn't leave you . . . it suffers exile with you! . . . Oh! how hard it is to live, to remain on this earth of bitterness and anguish. . . . But, tomorrow . . . in an hour, we shall be at port, what joy! Ah, what a good it will be to contemplate Jesus *face to face* all through the *whole* of eternity! Always, always more love, always more intoxicating joys . . . a happiness without clouds. . . .

What has Jesus done, then, to detach our souls from all that is created? Ah, he has struck a big blow . . . but it is a blow of love. God is admirable, but he is especially lovable; let us love him, then . . . let us love him enough to suffer for him all that he wills, even spiritual pains, aridities, anxieties, apparent coldness. . . . Ah, here is great love, to love Jesus without feeling the sweetness of this love . . . this is martyrdom. . . . Well, then, *let us die as martyrs.* Oh! Céline . . . sweet echo of my soul, do you understand? . . . Unknown martyrdom, known to God alone, which the eye of the creature cannot discover, a martyrdom without honor, without triumph. . . . That is love pushed to the point of heroism. . . . But, one day, a grateful God will cry out: "Now, my turn." Oh, what will we see then? . . . What is this life which will no more have an end? . . . God will be the soul of our soul . . . unfathomable mystery. . . . The eye of man has not seen the *uncreated* light, his ear has not heard the incomparable harmonies, and his heart cannot have any idea of what God reserves for those whom he loves (see 1 Cor 2:9). And all this will come *soon,* yes, soon. Let us hurry to fashion our crown; let us stretch forth our hand to seize the palm. And if we love much, if we love Jesus with a passion, he will

not be so cruel as to leave us for a long time on this earth of exile. . . .
Céline, during the *short moments* that *remain to us,* let us not lose our
time . . . let us save souls . . . souls are being lost like flakes of snow, and
Jesus weeps, and we . . . we are thinking of our sorrow without consoling
our Fiancé. . . . Oh, Céline, let us live for souls . . . let us be apostles . . .
let us save especially the souls of priests; these souls should be more
transparent than crystal. . . . Alas, how many bad priests, priests who are
not holy enough. . . . Let us pray, let us suffer for them, and, on the last
day, Jesus will be grateful. We shall give him souls! . . .
      Céline, do you understand the cry of my soul? . . . Together . . .
together, always, Céline and Thérèse of the Child Jesus

of the Holy Face
nov.carm.ind.

(L 94, to Céline)

J. M. J. T.

October 15, 1889

Jesus †

My dear Céline,
      If you only knew how you touched the heart of your Thérèse! . . . Your
little flowerpots are *delightful,* and you *don't know* the pleasure they gave
me! . . . Céline. . . Your letter pleased me very much; I felt how much our
souls were made to understand each other, and to walk by the same way!
. . . Life . . . ah, it's true, for us it has no more attraction . . . but I am
mistaken. It's true that the attractions of this world have vanished for us,
but this is only a smoke . . . and the *reality* remains for us. Yes, life is a
treasure . . . each moment is an *eternity,* an eternity of joy in heaven, an
eternity of seeing God *face to face,* of being one with him! . . . There is
only Jesus who *is;* all the rest *is not.* . . . Let us love him, then, unto folly;
let us save souls for him. Ah! Céline, I feel that Jesus is asking *both of us*
to quench *his thirst* by giving him souls, the souls of *priests* especially. I
feel that Jesus wills that I say this to you, for our mission is *to forget*
ourselves and to reduce ourselves to nothing. . . . We are so insignificant
. . . and yet Jesus wills that the salvation of *souls* depends on the sacrifices
of our love. He is begging souls from us. . . . Ah, let us understand his
look! There are so few who understand it. Jesus is giving us the remark-

able grace of instructing us himself and of showing us a *hidden light!* . . .
Céline . . . life will be short, eternity is without end. . . . Let us make our
life a continual sacrifice, a martyrdom of love, in order to console Jesus.
He wants only a *look,* a *sigh,* but a look and a sigh that are for *him alone!*
. . . Let all the moments of our life be for *him alone;* let creatures touch
us only in passing. There is only one thing to do during the night, the one
night of life which will come only once, and this is to love, to love Jesus
with all the strength of our heart and to save souls for him so that he may
be *loved.* . . . Oh, make Jesus loved! Céline! how easily I talk with you
. . . it's as if I were speaking to my soul. . . . Céline, it seems to me that I
can say everything to you. . . .

  (Thank you again for your pretty jars; little Jesus is *radiant* when he
is so well adorned.)

Sister Thérèse
of the Child Jesus
of the Holy Face
nov.carm.ind.

(L 96, to Céline)

J. M. J. T.

Carmel, July 18, 1890

Jesus †! . . .

Dear Céline,
  If you only knew what your letter said to my soul! . . . Ah! joy
inundated my heart like a vast ocean! . . . Céline, you know all that I have
to say to you since you are myself. . . . I'm sending you a page which says
much to my soul, and it seems to me your soul, too, will be immersed in
it. . . .
  Céline, it's *such a long time ago* . . . and already the soul of the prophet
Isaias was immersed, just as our own soul is, in the *hidden beauties* of
Jesus. . . . Ah, Céline, when I read these things, I wonder what time really
is? . . . Time is only a mirage, a dream . . . already God *sees us in glory,*
he *takes delight* in *our eternal beatitude!* Ah! what good this thought does
my soul, and I understand now why he is not bargaining with us. . . . He
feels that we *understand* him, and he is treating us as his friends, as his
dearest spouses. . . .

Céline, since Jesus was (alone in treading the wine) (see Is 63:3) which he is giving us to drink, let us not refuse in our turn to wear clothing stained in blood . . . let us tread for Jesus a new wine which may quench his thirst, which will return him love for love. Ah, let us not keep back one drop of wine that we can offer him . . . and, then, looking about (see Is 63:5), he will see that we are coming to help him! . . . His face was as though hidden (see Ps 53:3)! . . . Céline, it is still hidden today, for who understands the tears of Jesus? . . .

Dear Céline, let us make a little tabernacle in our heart where Jesus may take refuge, and then he will be consoled, and he will forget what we cannot forget: (the ingratitude of souls that abandon him in a deserted tabernacle! . . .)

(Open to me, my sister, my beloved, for my face is covered with dew, my locks with the drops of night) . . . (Sg 5:2). That is what Jesus says to our soul when he is abandoned and forgotten! . . . Céline, *forgetfulness,* it seems to me that it's this which causes him the greatest sorrow! . . .

Papa! . . . Ah, Céline, I cannot tell you all I am thinking, it would take too long, and how say things that the mind itself can hardly express, deep things that are in the innermost recesses of the soul! . . .

Jesus has sent us the best chosen cross that he was able to find in his immense love . . . how can we complain when he himself was looked upon as a man struck by God and humbled (Is 53:4)! . . . The divine charm delights my soul and consoles it in a marvelous way, at each moment of the day! . . . Ah, *the tears of Jesus, what smiles!* . . .

Kiss everybody for me, and tell them *all I would like to say!* . . . I think very much about my dear Léonie, my dear little Visitandine. Tell Marie of the Blessed Sacrament that Jesus asks much love from her, he wants from her reparation for the coldness he receives, and her heart must be a furnace in which Jesus may warm himself! . . . She must forget herself entirely in order to think only of him. . . .

Céline, let us pray for priests, ah, pray for them. May our life be consecrated for them; Jesus makes me feel every day that he wills this from the both of us.

C. T.*

(L 108, to Céline)

---

* The C. and T. are written under the words "the both of us."

The refectory, which I was given charge of immediately after I received the habit, furnished me, on more than one occasion, with the chance of putting my self-love in its proper place, i.e., under my feet. It's true, I had the great consolation of having the same task as you, dear Mother, and of being able to study your virtues at close range, but this closeness was the source of great suffering. I did not feel, *as formerly,* free to say everything to you, for there was the Rule to observe. I was unable to confide in you; after all, I was in *Carmel* and no longer at *Les Buissonnets* under the *paternal roof!*

The Blessed Virgin, nevertheless, was helping me prepare the dress of my soul; as soon as this dress was completed all the obstacles went away by themselves. The bishop sent me the permission I had sought, the community voted to receive me, and my profession was fixed for *September 8, 1890.*

Everything I have just written in so few words would require many detailed pages, but these pages will never be read on this earth. Very soon, dear Mother, I shall speak to you about everything in *our paternal home,* in that beautiful heaven toward which the sighs of our hearts rise!

My wedding dress was finally ready. It had been enriched by some *old* jewels given me by my Bridegroom, but this didn't satisfy his liberality. He wanted to give me a *new* diamond containing numberless rays. Papa's trial, with all its sad circumstances, made up the *old* jewels, and the *new* one was a trial, small in appearance, but one that caused me to suffer intensely.

(*Story,* VII)

I should have spoken to you about the retreat preceding my profession, dear Mother, before speaking about the trial I have mentioned; it was far from bringing me any consolations since the most absolute aridity and almost total abandonment were my lot. Jesus was sleeping as usual in my little boat; ah! I see very well how rarely souls allow him to sleep peacefully within them. Jesus is so fatigued with always having to take the initiative and to attend to others that he hastens to take advantage of the repose I offer to him. He will undoubtedly awaken before my great eternal retreat, but instead of being troubled about it this only gives me extreme pleasure.

Really, I am far from being a saint, and what I have just said is proof of this; instead of rejoicing, for example, at my aridity, I should attribute it to my little fervor and lack of fidelity; I should be desolate for having slept (for seven years) during my hours of prayer and my *thanksgivings* after holy communion; well, I am not desolate. I remember that *little children* are as pleasing to their parents when they are asleep as well as when they are wide awake; I remember, too, that when they perform operations, doctors put their patients to sleep. Finally, I remember that: *"The Lord knows our weakness, that he is mindful that we are but dust and ashes"* (Ps 102:14).

Just as all those that followed it, my profession retreat was one of great aridity. God showed me clearly, however, without my perceiving it, the way to please him and to practice the most sublime virtues. I have frequently noticed that Jesus doesn't want me to lay up *provisions*; he nourishes me at each moment with a totally new food; I find it within me without my knowing how it is there. I believe it is Jesus himself hidden in the depths of my poor little heart: he is giving me the grace of acting within me, making me think of all he desires me to do at the present moment.

A few days before my profession, I had the happiness of receiving the Sovereign Pontiff's blessing. I had requested it through good Brother Simeon for both *Papa* and myself, and it was a great consolation to be able to return to my dear little father the grace he obtained for me when taking me with him to Rome.

The *beautiful day* of my wedding finally arrived. It was without a single cloud; however, the preceding evening a storm arose within my soul the like of which I'd never seen before. Not a single doubt concerning my vocation had ever entered my mind until then, and it evidently was necessary that I experience this trial. In the evening, while making the way of the cross after Matins, my vocation appeared to me as a *dream*, a chimera. I found life in Carmel to be very beautiful, but the devil inspired me with the assurance that it wasn't for me and that I was misleading my superiors by advancing on this way to which I wasn't called. The darkness was so great that I could see and understand one thing only: I didn't have a vocation. Ah! how can I possibly describe the anguish in my soul? It appeared to me (and this is an absurdity which shows it was a temptation from the devil) that if I were to tell my novice mistress about these fears, she would prevent me from pronouncing my vows. And still I wanted to do God's will and return to the world rather than remain in Carmel and do my own will. I made the mistress come out of the choir and, filled with confusion, I told her the state of my soul. Fortunately, she saw things much clearer than I did, and she completely reassured me. The act of humility I had just performed put the devil to flight since he had perhaps thought that I would not dare admit my temptation. My doubts left me completely as soon as I finished speaking; nevertheless, to make my act of humility even more perfect, I still wished to confide my strange temptation to our Mother Prioress, who simply laughed at me.

In the morning of September 8, I felt as though I were flooded with a river of peace, and it was in this peace "which surpasses all understanding" (Phil 4:7) that I pronounced my holy vows. My union with Jesus was effected not in the midst of thunder and lightning, that is, in extraordinary graces, but in the bosom of a light breeze similar to the one our father St. Elias heard on the Mount (1 Kgs 19:12-13). What graces I begged for on that day! I really felt I was the queen and so I profited from my title by delivering captives, by obtaining favors from the *King* for his ungrateful subjects, finally, I wanted to deliver all the souls from purgatory and convert all sinners. I prayed very much for my *mother,* my dear sisters, my whole family, but especially for my poor father, who was so tried and so saintly. I offered myself to Jesus in order to accomplish his will perfectly in me without creatures ever being able to place any obstacle in the way.

(Story, VIII)

The Trials of Love

1890–1895

Thérèse's father was to continue his humiliation and martyrdom up to his death on July 29, 1894, first in a psychiatric hospital at Caen for three years, and then back in Lisieux for two more years. It was Céline who remained at his side and we see from the letters of Thérèse to her how she needed encouragement. Thérèse's affection for her was now "a mother's love rather than a sister's." Thérèse suffered greatly because she feared lest Céline should "give her heart to a mortal being." She could not accept "her not being the spouse of Jesus."

The year after her profession, Thérèse was having "great interior trials of all kinds, even to the point of asking myself whether heaven really existed" (*Story*, p. 173). But at the retreat that year, the director, Fr. Alexis Prou, launched her "full sail upon the waves of confidence and love," in particular by assuring her that her faults caused God no pain. This was a new light for her, but one that would henceforth guide her life. She writes to Céline in July 1893: "I am not always faithful, but I never get discouraged; I abandon myself into the arms of Jesus." Another factor which gave fresh impetus to her fervor was the election of her sister, Pauline, to the office of prioress on February 20, 1893: "Since the blessed day of your election . . . I have flown in the ways of love" (*Story*, p. 174). Yet this election was the cause of suffering, too, because she met with opposition from the former prioress, Mother de Gonzague. Addressing Pauline, Thérèse says: "What an abundant harvest you have reaped! You have sown in tears, but soon you will see the result of your works, and you will return filled with joy, carrying your sheaves" (*ibid.*).

There is a marked change in the spiritual life of Thérèse during these years. We notice that while suffering and death still hold an attraction for her, she no longer desires them. "It is love alone that attracts me," and she now has no other desire than "to love Jesus unto folly." There is also a great longing for the hidden life; she wants to hide herself from all eyes except those of her Beloved, so that he can always turn to her and find that he is known and understood. "Let us remain hidden in our divine Flower of the fields," she urges Céline (Letter 142). More and more she was becoming aware of the importance of "nothings" in showing love for Jesus. It was not necessary to do dazzling deeds or be famous but to carry out God's will with love. Without love all works are nothing, but with love even these nothings—a word or a smile—"please Jesus more than the mastery of the world or martyrdom suffered with generosity" (Letter 143).

In her younger days she kept a sort of balance-sheet of her acts. But now her acts "are not for the purpose of weaving my crown, gaining merits; it is in order to please Jesus" (*ibid.*). Not that she is opposed to acts of virtue for those who are so counselled by their directors, "but my director, who is Jesus, teaches me not to count up my acts. He teaches me to do all through love, to refuse him nothing, to be content when he gives me a chance of proving to him that I love him. But this is done in peace, in abandonment; it is Jesus who is doing all in me, and I am doing nothing" (Letter 142).

Here is the other great discovery—abandonment. Merit does not consist in doing or in giving much, but rather in receiving, in loving much: "Perfection consists in doing his will, and the soul that surrenders itself totally to him is called by Jesus himself 'his mother,' 'his sister,' and his family." Thérèse need not be concerned now with examining her faults too much; she must profit from everything, from the good and the bad she finds in herself, leaving Jesus to be the "banker": "What she must do is abandon herself, surrender herself, without keeping anything, even the joy of knowing how much the bank is returning to her" (*ibid.*).

Saving souls was always foremost in her vocation, and in the text of John 4:35, "lift up your eyes . . ." she sees a call to prayer for the salvation of souls: "See how in my heaven there are empty places; it is up to you to fill them, you are my Moses praying on the mountain, ask me for workers and I shall send them, I await only a prayer, a sigh from your heart! . . . Our mission as Carmelites is to form evangelical workers who will save thousands of souls whose mothers we shall be" (Letter 135).

As one who had always seen the graces she had received as an expression of God's mercy, it was only natural that she should want to dedicate herself totally to this merciful love: "I feel in my heart immense desires and it is with confidence I ask you to come and take possession of my soul. . . . I do not want to lay up merits for heaven. I want to work for your love alone with the one purpose of pleasing you, consoling your sacred heart, and saving souls who will love you eternally" (Act of Oblation to Merciful Love, June 11, 1895).

Her Resignation to Love

The year which followed my profession, that is, two months before Mother Geneviève's death, I received great graces during my retreat. Ordinarily, the retreats which are preached are more painful to me than the ones I make alone, but this year it was otherwise. I had made a preparatory novena with great fervor, in spite of the inner sentiment I had, for it seemed to me that the preacher would not be able to understand me since he was supposed to do good to great sinners but not to religious souls. God wanted to show me that he was the director of my soul, and so he made use of this Father specifically, who was appreciated only by me in the community. At the time I was having great interior trials of all kinds, even to the point of asking myself whether heaven really existed. I felt disposed to say nothing of my interior dispositions since I didn't know how to express them, but I had hardly entered the confessional when I felt my soul expand. After speaking only a few words, I *was understood* in a marvelous way and my soul was like a book in which this priest read better than I did myself. He launched me full sail upon the waves of *confidence and love* which so strongly attracted me, but upon which I dared not advance. He told me that *my faults caused God no pain, and that holding as he did God's place,* he was telling me *in his name* that God was very much pleased with me.

Oh! how happy I was to hear those consoling words! Never had I heard that our faults *could not cause God any pain,* and this assurance filled me with joy, helping me to bear patiently with life's exile. I felt at the bottom of my heart that this was really so, for God is more tender than a mother, and were you not, dear Mother, always ready to pardon the little offenses I committed against you involuntarily? How often I experienced this! No word of reproach touched me as much as did one of your caresses. My nature was such that fear made me recoil; with *love* not only did I advance, I actually *flew*.

(*Story*, VIII)

J. M. J. T.

Jesus †

Carmel, April 26, 1891

Dear Céline,

For the fourth time Thérèse is coming from the solitude of Carmel to wish you a happy birthday. . . . Oh! how these wishes little resemble those of the world. . . . It is not health, happiness, fortune, glory, etc., that Thérèse desires for her Céline; oh, no, it is exile; our heart is there where our treasure is (see Mt 6:21), and our treasure is up above in the homeland where Jesus prepares a place (see Jn 14:2) near himself. I say *one place* and not places, for no doubt the same throne is reserved to those who on earth have always been only one soul. . . . Together we grew up; together Jesus instructed us in his secrets, sublime secrets that he hides from the mighty and reveals to the little ones (see Mt 11:25); together we suffered at *Rome.* Our hearts were closely united then, and life on earth might have been the ideal of happiness if Jesus had not come to make our bonds even tighter. Yes, by separating us, he has united us in a way unknown up to that time to my soul, for since that moment I can desire nothing for myself alone but for us both. . . . Ah, Céline! . . . Three years ago our souls had not yet been broken; happiness was still possible for us on earth, but Jesus cast a glance of love on us, a glance veiled in tears, and this glance has become for us an ocean of suffering, but also an ocean of graces and love. He took from us the one whom we loved with so much tenderness, in a way still more painful than when he had taken from us our dear mother in the springtime of our life. But was it not so that we could truly say, "Our Father, who art in heaven?" Oh! how consoling are these words, what infinite horizons they open to our eyes. . . . Céline, the foreign land has for us only wild plants and thorns, but is this not the portion it has given to our divine Spouse? Oh! how beautiful for us too is this portion that is ours, and who will tell us what eternity reserves for us? . . . Dear Céline, you who used to ask me so many questions when we were little, I wonder how it happened that you had never asked me this question: "Why did God not create me an angel?" Ah, Céline, I shall tell you what I think. If Jesus did not create you an angel in heaven, it is because he wants you to be an angel on earth; yes, Jesus wants to have his heavenly court here below just as up above! He wants angel-martyrs, he wants angel-apostles, and he has created a little unknown flower, who is named

Céline, with this intention in mind. He wills that his little flower save souls for him; for this, he wills only one thing: that his flower *look at* him while suffering her martyrdom. . . . And it is this mysterious look exchanged between Jesus and his little flower that will effect marvels and will give Jesus a multitude of other flowers (above all, a certain lily faded and withered, which he will have to change into a rose of love and repentance!) . . .

Dear Céline, do not be vexed if I tell you that up above we would have the same place, for, do you not see, I think that a poor little daisy can really grow in the same soil as a beautiful lily dazzling in its whiteness, or, again, a little pearl can be mounted by the side of a diamond and borrow its brilliance from it! . . .

Oh! Céline, let us love Jesus to infinity, and from our two hearts let us make only one so that it may be greater in love! . . .

Céline, I shall never come to an end with you; understand all I would like to tell you for your twenty-two years! . . .

Your little sister who is only one with you. . . .

(Do you know that we two are now forty years old. It is not surprising that we have already experienced so many things. What do you think of that?)

Thérèse of the Child of Jesus
of the Holy Face
nov. carm. ind.

(L 127, to Céline)

J. M. J. T.

July 8, 1891

Jesus †

Dear Céline,

Your short note spoke volumes to my soul; it was for me like a faithful echo repeating all my own thoughts. . . .

Our dear mother is still very sick; it is sad to see those whom we love suffering in this way. However, do not be too grieved; though Jesus intends to enjoy in heaven our dear mother's presence, he will be unable to refuse to leave on earth her whose maternal hand can lead and console us so well in the exile of life. . . . Oh! what an exile it is, the exile of earth,

especially during these hours when everything seems to abandon us. . . .
But it is then that it is precious, it is then that the day of salvation dawns
(see 2 Cor 6:2); yes, dear Céline, suffering alone can give birth to souls
for Jesus. . . . Is it surprising that we are so favored, we whose only desire
is to save a soul that seems to be lost forever? . . .* The details interested
me very much, while making my heart beat very fast. . . . But I shall give
you some other details that are not any more consoling. The unfortunate
prodigal went to Coutances where he started over again the conferences
given at Caen. It appears he intends to travel throughout France in this
way. . . . Céline. . . And with all this, they add that it is easy to see that
remorse is gnawing at him. He goes into the churches with a huge crucifix,
and he seems to be making great acts of adoration. . . . His wife follows
him everywhere. Dear Céline, he is really culpable, more culpable than
any other sinner ever was who was converted. But cannot Jesus do once
what he has not yet ever done? And if he were not to desire it, would he
have placed in the heart of his poor little spouses a desire that he could
not realize? . . . No, it is certain that he desires more than we do to bring
back this poor stray sheep to the fold. A day will come when he will open
his eyes, and then who knows whether France will not be traversed by
him with a totally different goal from the one he has in mind now? Let us
not grow tired of prayer; confidence works miracles. And Jesus said to
Blessed Margaret Mary: *"One just soul* has so much power over my heart
that it can obtain pardon for a thousand *criminals."* No one knows if one

---

* Père Loyson—Fr. Hyacinthe Loyson unsuccessfully tried his vocation with the
Sulpicians and Dominicans before he joined the Carmelite Order where he became
provincial superior. In 1869 he left the Church and three years later he married a
young American widow, a Protestant, by whom he had a son. In 1879 he founded
the Catholic Gallican Church which rejected papal infallibility (which had just been
defined by Vatican Council I), proposed the election of bishops by priests and
lay-people, was in favor of a married clergy and wanted the liturgy in French.
Despite being excommunicated, he continued lecturing throughout France. In 1891
he was in Normandy and Thérèse read about him in some newspaper cuttings
supplied to her by Céline. While others referred to Fr. Loyson as a "renegade,"
Thérèse always called him her "brother." She prayed for him right up to her death
and offered her last communion for him on August 19, 1897. In January 1911 the
Lisieux Carmel sent him a copy of *Story of a Soul.* Acknowledging the book he
said: "I was touched, very touched indeed, by many of the things I read in the book."
However, it did not effect his conversion. During his last illness Père Loyson asked
the archpriest of the Armenians in Paris, Msgr. Kibarian, to visit him, and the latter
administered the last rites to him in the Armenian rite. He died on February 9, 1912,
whispering "My sweet Jesus!"

is just or sinful, but, Céline, Jesus gives us the grace of feeling at the bottom of our heart that we would prefer to die rather than to offend him; and then it is not our merits but those of our Spouse, which are *ours,* that we offer to our Father who is in heaven, in order that our brother, a son of the Blessed Virgin, return vanquished to throw himself beneath the mantle of the most merciful of Mothers. . . . Dear Céline, I am obliged to end; divine the rest, there remain *volumes* to be divined! . . .

Kiss everybody for me, and all that you would like to tell them as coming from me is what I am thinking! . . .

Thérèse of the Child Jesus
of the Holy Face

(L 129, to Céline)

The Darkness of Night

J. M. J. T.

August 15, 1892

Jesus †

Dear Céline,

I cannot allow the letter [of Sister Agnes of Jesus] to leave without joining a note to it. For this, I must steal a few moments from Jesus, but he does not hold it against me, for it is about him that we speak together, without him no discourse has any charms for our hearts. . . . Céline, the vast solitudes, the enchanting horizons opening up before you must be speaking volumes to your soul. I myself see nothing of all that, but I say with Saint John of the Cross: "My Beloved is the mountains, and lonely, wooded valleys, etc." (*Spiritual Canticle,* st. 14). And this Beloved instructs my soul, he speaks to it in silence, in darkness. . . . Recently, there came a thought to me which I have to tell my Céline. It was one day when I was thinking of what I could do to save souls, a word of the gospel gave me a real light. In days gone by, Jesus said to his disciples when showing them the fields of ripe corn: "Lift up your eyes and see how the

fields are already white enough to be harvested" (Jn 4:35), and a little later: "In truth, the harvest is abundant but the number of laborers is small, ask then the master of the harvest to send laborers" (Mt 9:37-38). What a mystery! . . . Is not Jesus all-powerful? Are not creatures his who made them? Why, then, does Jesus say: "Ask the Lord of the harvest that he send some workers?" Why? . . . Ah! it is because Jesus has so incomprehensible a love for us that he wills that we have a share with him in the salvation of souls. He wills to do nothing without us. The Creator of the universe awaits the prayer of a poor little soul to save other souls redeemed like it at the price of all his blood. Our own vocation is not to go out to harvest the fields of ripe corn. Jesus does not say to us: "*Lower* your eyes, look at the fields and go harvest them." Our mission is still more sublime. These are the words of our Jesus: "*Lift* your eyes and see."
See how in my heaven there are empty places; it is up to you to fill them, you are my Moses praying on the mountain, ask me for workers and I shall send them, I await only a prayer, a sigh from your heart! . . .

Is not the apostolate of prayer, so to speak, more elevated than that of the word? Our mission as Carmelites is to form evangelical workers who will save thousands of souls whose mothers we shall be. . . . Céline, if these were not the very words of our Jesus, who would dare to believe in them? . . . I find that our share is really beautiful, what have we to envy in priests? . . . How I would like to be able to tell you all I am thinking, but time is lacking, understand all I could write you! . . .

On the feast day of Jeanne, wish her a happy feast for us with a little bouquet. The Rule does not permit us to do it, but tell her that we shall be thinking even more of her. Kiss everybody for me, and tell them all the nicest things you can think of. If you were to find some heather, I would be pleased.

> Your little Thérèse
> of the Child Jesus
> rel. carm. ind.
>
> (L 135, to Céline)

J. M. J. T.

Jesus †

Carmel, October 19, 1892

Dear Céline,

Formerly, in the days of our childhood, we used to enjoy our feast because of the little gifts we mutually exchanged. The smallest object had then an incomparable value in our eyes. . . . Soon, the scene changed. Wings grew on the youngest of the birds, and it flew away far from the sweet nest of its childhood, and all illusion vanished! Summer had followed spring, life's reality, the dreams of youth. . . .

Céline, was it not at that decisive moment that the bonds which joined our hearts were tightened? Yes, separation united us in a way that language cannot express. Our childlike affection was changed into a union of feelings, a unity of souls and minds. Who, then, could have accomplished this marvel? . . . Ah! it was he who had ravished our hearts. "The Beloved chosen among thousands, the odor alone of his ointments suffices to draw us after him (see Sg 5:10; 1:3-4). Following his steps, young maidens run lightly on the road . . ." (*Spiritual Canticle*, st. 25).

Jesus has attracted us together, although by different ways; together he has raised us above all the fragile things of this world whose image passes away (see 1 Cor 7:31). He has placed, so to speak, *all things* under our feet. Like Zacchaeus, we climbed a tree to see Jesus (see Lk 19:4). . . . Then we could say with Saint John of the Cross: "All is mine, all is for me, the earth is mine, the heavens are mine, God is mine, and the Mother of my God is mine" (*Prayer of a soul enkindled by love*). With regard to the Blessed Virgin, I must confide to you one of my simple ways with her. I surprise myself at times by saying to her: "But good Blessed Virgin, I find I am more blessed than you, for I have you for Mother, and you do not have a *Blessed Virgin to love*. . . . It is true you are the Mother of Jesus, but this Jesus you have given entirely to us . . . and he, on the cross, he gave you to us as Mother. Thus we are richer than you since we possess Jesus and since you are ours also. Formerly, in your humility, you wanted one day to be the little servant of the happy Virgin who would have the honor of being the Mother of God, and here I am, a poor little creature, and I am not your servant but your child. You are the Mother of Jesus, and you are my Mother." No doubt, the Blessed Virgin must laugh at my simplicity, and nevertheless what I am telling her is really true! . . . Céline, what a mystery is our grandeur in Jesus. . . . This is all that Jesus has shown us in making us climb the symbolic tree about which I was just talking to you. And now what science is he about to teach us? Has he not taught us all? . . . Let us listen to what he is saying to us: "Make haste to descend, I must lodge today at your house" (Lk 19:5). Well, Jesus tells us to descend. . . . Where, then, must we descend? Céline, you know better than I, however, let me tell you where we must now follow Jesus. In days gone by, the Jews asked our divine Savior: "Master, where do you live?" (Jn 1:38). And he answered: "The foxes have their lairs, the birds of heaven their nests, but I have no place to rest my head" (Mt 8:20). This is where we must descend in order that we may serve as an abode for Jesus. To be so poor that we do not have a place to rest our head. This is, dear Céline, what Jesus has done in my soul during my retreat. . . . You understand, there is question here of the interior. Besides, has not the exterior already been reduced to nothing by means of the very sad trial of Caen? . . . In our dear father, Jesus has stricken us in the most sensitive exterior part of our heart; now let us allow him to act, he can complete his work in our souls. . . . What Jesus desires is that we receive him into our hearts. No doubt, they are already empty of creatures, but, alas, I feel mine is not entirely empty of myself, and it is for this reason that Jesus tells me to descend. . . . He, the King of kings, humbled himself in such a way that his face was hidden (see Is 53:3), and no one recognized him . . . and I, too, want to hide my face, I want my Beloved alone to see it, that he be the only one to count my tears . . . that in my heart at least he may rest his dear head and feel that there he is known and understood! . . .

Céline, I cannot tell you all I would like, my soul is powerless. . . . Ah, if only I could! . . . But, no, this is not in my power . . . why be sad, do you not always think what I am thinking? . . . Thus all I do not tell you, you divine. Jesus makes you feel it in your heart. Has he not, moreover, set up his abode there to console himself for the crimes of sinners? Yes, it is there in the intimate retreat of the soul that he instructs us together, and one day he will show us the day which will no longer have any setting. . . .

Happy feast. How sweet it will be one day for your Thérèse to wish it to you in heaven! . . .

(L 137, to Céline)

Some Rest in the Valley

J. M. J. T.

Carmel, July 6, 1893

Jesus †

Dear Céline,

Your two letters were like a sweet melody for my heart. . . . I am happy to see Jesus' predilection for my Céline. How he loves her, how he *looks tenderly* upon her! . . . Now here we are, all five of us, on our way. What joy to be able to say: "I am sure of doing God's will." This holy will is clearly manifested with regard to Céline. She is the one whom Jesus has *chosen* among us all to be the crown, the reward of the holy patriarch who has delighted heaven by his fidelity. How dare you say you have been forgotten, less loved than the others? I say you have *been chosen* by privilege, your mission is all the more beautiful because, while remaining our dear father's visible angel, you are at the same time the spouse of Jesus. This is true, perhaps Céline thinks, but I am doing less than the others for God. I have more consolations and consequently less merits. "My thoughts are not your thoughts," says the Lord (Is 55:8). Merit does not consist in doing or in giving much, but rather in receiving, in loving much. . . . It is said, it is much sweeter to give than to receive (see Acts 20:35), and it is true. But when Jesus wills to take *for himself the sweetness of giving*, it would not be gracious to refuse. Let us allow him to take and give all he wills. Perfection consists in doing his will, and the soul that surrenders itself totally to him is called by Jesus himself "his mother, his sister," and his whole family (see Mt 12:5). And elsewhere: "If anyone loves me, he will keep my word (that is, he will do my will) and my Father will love him, and we will come to him and make our abode with him" (see Jn 14:23). Oh, Céline how easy it is to please Jesus, to delight his heart, one has only to love him, without looking at one's self, without examining one's faults too much. Your Thérèse is not in the heights at this moment, but Jesus is teaching her to learn "to draw profit from everything, *from the good* and *the bad* she finds in herself." He is teaching her to play at the bank of love, or rather he plays for her and does not tell her how he goes about it, for that is his affair and not Thérèse's. What she must do is abandon herself, surrender herself, without keeping anything, not even the joy of knowing how much the bank is returning to her. But after all she is not the prodigal child, it is not worthwhile for Jesus to set a banquet for her "since she is always with him" (see Lk 15:31). Our Lord wills to leave the faithful sheep in the desert (see Mt 18:12). How much this says to me! . . . He is *sure to them*; they could no longer go astray, for they are captives of love. So Jesus takes away his tangible presence from them to order to give his consolations to sinners. If he does lead them to Tabor, it is for a few moments, the valley is most frequently the place of his repose. "It is there he takes his rest at midday" (Sg 1:7). The morning of our life has passed, we have enjoyed the perfumed breezes of the dawn. Then everything smiled at us, Jesus was making us feel his sweet presence, but when the sun became hot, the Beloved led us into his garden, he made us gather the *myrrh* of trial by separating us from *everything* and from himself. The hill of myrrh has strengthened us with its bitter scents, so Jesus has made us come down again, and now we are in the valley. He leads us beside the waters (see Ps 22:2). . . . Dear Céline, I do not know too well what I am saying to you, but it seems you will understand, divine what I would like to say. Ah! let us be always Jesus' *drop of dew*. In that is happiness, perfection. . . . Fortunately, I am speaking to you, for other persons would be unable to understand my language, and I admit it is true for only a few souls. In fact, directors have others advance in perfection by having them perform a great number of acts of virtue, and they are right; but my director, who is Jesus, teaches me not to count up my acts. He teaches me to do *all* through love, to refuse him nothing, to be content when he gives me a chance of proving to him that I love him. But this is done in peace, in *abandonment,* it is Jesus who is doing all in me, and I am doing nothing.

I feel very much united to my Céline. I believe God has not often made two souls who understand each other so well, never a discordant note. The hand of Jesus touching one of the lyres makes the other vibrate at the same time. . . . Oh! let us remain hidden in our divine Flower of the fields until the shadows lengthen (see Sg 4:6); let us allow the drops of *liqueur* to be appreciated by creatures. Since we are pleasing *our lily,* let us remain joyfully his drop, his *single* drop of dew! . . . And to this drop that has consoled him during the exile, what will he not give us in the homeland? . . . He tells us himself: "He who is thirsty, let him come *to me* and drink" (Jn 7:37), and so Jesus is and will be our *ocean.* . . . Like the thirsty hind we long for this water (see Ps 41:2) that is promised to us, but our consolation is great: to be the ocean of Jesus also, the ocean of the lily of the valleys! . . . Your heart alone will be able to read this letter, for I myself have difficulty in deciphering it. I have no more ink, I was obliged *to spit* into our inkwell to make some . . . is this not something to laugh about? I kiss the whole family, but especially my dear king, who will receive a kiss from my Céline from his queen.

Sister Thérèse
of the Child Jesus
of the Holy Face
rel. carm. ind.

(L 142, to Céline)

J. M. J. T.

Carmel, July 18, 1893

Jesus †

Dear Céline,

I was not counting on answering your letter this time, but our Mother wants me to add a note to hers. What things I would have to tell you! But since I have only a few moments, I must first assure the little drop of dew that her Thérèse understands her. . . . After having read your letter, I went to prayer, and taking the gospel, I asked Jesus to find a passage for you, and this is what I found: "Behold the fig tree and the other trees, when they begin to bear tender leaves, you judge that summer is near. In the same way, when you will see these things taking place, know that the kingdom of God is near" (Lk 21:29). I closed the book, I had read enough; in fact, *these things* taking place in my Céline's soul prove the kingdom of Jesus is set up in her soul. . . . Now I want to tell you what is taking place in my *own* soul; no doubt, it is the same things as in yours. You have rightly said, Céline, the cool mornings have passed for us, there remain no more flowers to gather, Jesus has taken them for himself. Perhaps he will make new ones bloom one day, but in the meantime what must we do? Céline, God is no longer asking anything from me . . . in the beginning, he was asking an infinity of things from me. I thought, at times, that since Jesus was no longer asking anything from me, I had to go along quietly in peace and love, doing only what he was asking me. . . . But I had a light. St. Teresa says we must maintain love. *The wood* is not within our reach when we are in darkness, in aridities, but at least are we not obliged to throw little pieces of straw on it? Jesus is really powerful enough to keep the fire going by himself. However, he is satisfied when he sees us put a little fuel on it. This *attentiveness* pleases Jesus, and then he throws on the fire a lot of wood. We do not see it, but we do feel the *strength* of love's warmth. I have experienced it; when I *am feeling* nothing, when I am *incapable of praying,* of practicing virtue, then is the moment for seeking opportunities, *nothings*, which please Jesus more than mastery of the world or even martyrdom suffered with generosity. For example, a smile, a friendly word, when I would want to say nothing, or put on a look of annoyance, etc., etc.

Céline, do you understand? It is not for the purpose of weaving my crown, gaining merits, it is in order to please Jesus. . . . When I do not have any opportunities, I want at least to tell him frequently that I love him; this is not difficult, and it keeps the *fire* going. *Even though* this fire of love would seem to me to have gone out, I would like to throw something on it, and Jesus could then relight it. Céline, I am afraid I have not said what I should; perhaps you will think I always do what I am saying. Oh, no! I am not always faithful, but I never get discouraged; I abandon myself into the arms of Jesus. The little drop of dew goes deeper into the calyx of the flower of the fields, and there it finds again all it has lost and even much more.

Your little Sister Thérèse
of the Child Jesus
of the Holy Face
re. carm. ind.

(L 143, to Céline)

The Discovery of Mercy

J. M. J. T.

January 1895

Jesus †

It is to you, dear Mother, to you who are doubly my Mother, that I come to confide the story of my soul. The day you asked me to do this, it seemed to me it would distract my heart by too much concentration on myself, but since then Jesus has made me feel that in obeying simply, I would be pleasing him; besides, I'm going to be doing only one thing: I shall begin to sing what I must sing eternally: *"The Mercies of the Lord"* (Ps 88:2).

Before taking up my pen, I knelt before the statue of Mary (the one which has given so many proofs of the maternal preferences of heaven's Queen for our family), and I begged her to guide my hand that it trace no line displeasing to her. Then opening the holy gospels my eyes fell upon these words: "And going up a mountain, he called to him men of his own choosing, and they came to him" (Mk 3:13). This is the mystery of my vocation, my whole life, and especially the mystery of the privileges Jesus showered upon my soul. He does not call those who are worthy but those whom he pleases or as St. Paul says: "God will have mercy on whom he will have mercy, and he will show pity to whom he will show pity. So then there is question not of him who wills nor of him who runs, but of God showing mercy" (Rom 9:15-16).

I wondered for a long time why God has preferences, why all souls don't receive an equal amount of graces. I was surprised when I saw him shower his extraordinary favors on saints who had offended him, for instance, St. Paul and St. Augustine, and whom he forced, so to speak, to accept his graces. When reading the lives of the saints, I was puzzled at seeing how our Lord was pleased to caress certain ones from the cradle to the grave, allowing no obstacle in their way when coming to him, helping them with such favors that they were unable to soil the immaculate beauty of their baptismal robe. I wondered why poor savages died in great numbers without even having heard the name of God pronounced.

Jesus deigned to teach me this mystery. He set before me the book of nature; I understood how all the flowers he has created are beautiful, how the splendor of the rose and the whiteness of the lily do not take away the perfume of the little violet or the delightful simplicity of the daisy. I understood that if all flowers wanted to be roses, nature would lose her springtime beauty, and the fields would no longer be decked out with little wild flowers.

And so it is in the world of souls, Jesus' garden. He willed to create great souls comparable to lilies and roses, but he has created smaller ones and these must be content to be daisies or violets destined to give joy to God's glances when he looks down at his feet. Perfection consists in doing his will, in being what he wills us to be.

I understood, too, that our Lord's love is revealed as perfectly in the most simple soul that resists his grace in nothing as in the most excellent soul; in fact, since the nature of love is to humble oneself, if all souls resembled those of the holy Doctors who illumined the Church with the clarity of their teachings, it seems God would not descend so low when coming to their heart. But he created the child who knows only how to make his feeble cries heard; he has created the poor savage who has nothing but the natural law to guide him. It is to their hearts that God deigns to lower himself. These are the wild flowers whose simplicity attracts him. When coming down in this way, God manifests his infinite grandeur. Just as the sun shines simultaneously on the tall cedars and on each little flower as though it were alone on the earth, so our Lord is occupied particularly with each soul as though there were no others like it. And just as in nature all the seasons are arranged in such a way as to make the humblest daisy bloom on a set day, in the same way, everything works out for the good of each soul.

Perhaps you are wondering, dear Mother, with some astonishment where I am going from here, for up until now I've said nothing that resembles the story of my life. But you asked me to write under no constraint whatever would come into my mind. It is not, then, my life properly so called that I am going to write; it is my *thoughts* on the graces God deigned to grant me. I find myself at a period in my life when I can cast a glance upon the past; my soul has matured in the crucible of exterior and interior trials. And now, like a flower strengthened by the storm, I can raise my head and see the words of Psalm 22 realized in me: "The Lord is my Shepherd, I shall not want; he makes me lie down in green pastures. He leads me beside still waters; he restores my soul. Even though I walk through the valley of the shadow of death, I fear no evil; for thou art with me" (Ps 22:1-4). To me the Lord has always been "merciful and good, slow to anger and abounding in steadfast love" (Ps 102:8).

It is with great happiness, then, that I come to sing the mercies of the Lord with you, dear Mother. It is for *you alone* I am writing the story of the *little flower* gathered by Jesus. I will talk freely and without any worries as to the numerous digressions I will make. A mother's heart understands her child even when it can but stammer, and so I'm sure of being understood by you, who formed my heart, offering it up to Jesus!

It seems to me that if a little flower could speak, it would tell simply what God has done for it without trying to hide its blessings. It would not say, under the pretext of a false humility, it is not beautiful or without perfume, that the sun has taken away its splendor and the storm has broken its stem when it knows that all this is untrue.

(Story, I)

I had the happiness of contemplating for a long time the *marvels* Jesus is working by means of my dear Mother. I see that *suffering alone* gives birth to souls, and more than ever before these sublime words of Jesus unveil their depth to me: *"Amen, amen, I say to you, unless the grain of wheat falls into the ground and dies, it remains alone; but if it dies, it will bring forth much fruit"* (Jn 12:24). What an abundant harvest you have reaped! You have sown in tears, but soon you will see the result of your works, and you will return filled with joy, carrying sheaves in your arms (Ps 125:5-6). O Mother, among these ripe sheaves is hidden the little *white flower*; however, in heaven she will have a voice with which to sing of your *gentleness and your virtues* which she sees you practice every day in the darkness and the silence of life's exile!

Yes, for the past two years I have understood very well the mysteries hidden from me until then. God showed me the same mercy he showed to King Solomon. He has not willed that I have one single desire which is not fulfilled, not only my desires for perfection but those too whose vanity I *have understood* without having experienced it.

As I have always looked upon you, dear Mother, as my *ideal,* I desired to be like you in everything; when I saw you do beautiful paintings and delightful poems, I said to myself: How happy I would be if I were able to paint and to know how to express my thoughts in verse and thus do good to souls. I would not have wanted *to ask* for these natural gifts and my desires remained *hidden away* at the bottom of my *heart. Jesus hidden* also in this poor little heart was pleased to show it that *everything is vanity and affliction of spirit under the sun* (Eccl 2:11). To the great astonishment of the Sisters I was told to paint, and God permitted that I profit by the lessons my dear Mother gave me. He willed also that I write poems and compose little pieces which were considered beautiful. And just as Solomon, when he *considered all the works of his hands in which he had placed so much useless toil, saw that all is vanity and affliction of spirit,* in the same way I recognized from *experience* that happiness consists in hiding oneself, in remaining ignorant of created things. I understood that without *love* all works are nothing, even the most dazzling, such as raising the dead to life and converting peoples.

Instead of doing me any harm, of making me vain, the gifts which God showered upon me (without my having asked for them) drew me to *him*; and I saw that he alone was *unchangeable,* that he alone could fulfill my immense desires.

There are other desires of another kind that Jesus was pleased to grant me, childish desires similar to the snow at my reception of the habit.

You know, dear Mother, how much I love flowers; when making myself a prisoner at the age of fifteen, I gave up forever the pleasure of running through fields decked out in their springtime treasures. Well, never in my life did I possess so many flowers as after my entrance into Carmel. It is the custom for fiancés to often give their fiancées bouquets and Jesus didn't forget it. He sent me in great abundance sheaves of corn-flowers, huge daisies, poppies, etc., all the flowers that delighted me the most. There was even a little flower called corn-cockle which I had never found since our stay at Lisieux. I wanted very much to see it again, that flower of *my childhood* which I had picked in the fields of Alençon. And at Carmel it came to smile at me again and show me that in the smallest things as well as the greatest, God gives the hundredfold in this life to those souls who leave everything for love of him (see Mt 19:29).

But the most intimate of my desires, the greatest of them all, which I thought would never be realized, was my dear Céline's entrance into the same Carmel as ours. This *dream* appeared to be improbable: to live under the same roof, to share the joys and pains of the companion of my childhood; I had made my sacrifice complete by confiding to Jesus my dear sister's future, resolved to see her leave for the other side of the world if necessary. The only thing I couldn't accept was her not being the spouse of Jesus, for since I loved her as much as I loved myself it was impossible for me to see her give her heart to a mortal being. I had already suffered very much when knowing she was exposed to dangers in the world which were unknown to me. Since my entrance into Carmel, I can say that my affection for Céline was a mother's love rather than a sister's. When she was to attend a party one day, the very thought of it caused me so much pain that I begged God to *prevent her from dancing*, and (contrary to my custom) I even shed a torrent of tears. Jesus deigned to answer me. He permitted that his little fiancée *be unable to dance* that evening (even though she was not embarrassed to dance gracefully when it was necessary). She was invited to dance and was unable to refuse the invitation, but her partner found out he was totally powerless to make her dance; to his great confusion he was condemned simply to *walking* in order to conduct her to her place, and then he made his escape and did not reappear for the whole evening. This incident, unique in its kind, made me grow in confidence and love for the One who set *his seal* upon my forehead and had imprinted it at the same time upon that of my dear Céline.

Last year, July 29, God broke the bonds of his incomparable servant and called him to his eternal reward; at the same time he broke those which still held his dear fiancée in the world because she had accomplished her mission. Having been given the office of *representing us all* with our father whom we so tenderly loved, she had accomplished this mission just like an angel. And angels don't remain on earth once they've fulfilled God's will, for they return immediately to him, and this is why they're represented with wings. Our angel also spread her white wings; she was ready to fly *far away* to find Jesus, but he made her fly *close by*. He was content with simply accepting the great sacrifice which was very painful for little Thérèse. Her Céline had kept a secret hidden from her for *two full years.** Ah, how Céline herself had suffered because of this! Finally, from heaven my dear King, who never liked stragglers when he was still with us on earth, hastened to arrange Céline's muddled affairs, and she joined us on September 14!

When the difficulties seemed insurmountable one day, I said to Jesus during my act of thanksgiving: "You know, my God, how much I want to know whether Papa went *straight to heaven*; I am not asking you to speak to me, but give me a sign. If Sister A. of J. consents to Céline's entrance or places no obstacle to it, this will be an answer that Papa went

---

* Père Pichon, S. J., Marie's director, was sent to Canada as a missionary in 1884. Planning to set up a new group there, he invited Céline to join him to assist the new foundation, but he warned her not to tell anyone about it, least of all Thérèse who had her heart set on Céline's becoming a Carmelite. Céline faithfully kept the secret for two years.

straight to you." This Sister, as you are aware, dear Mother, found we were already too many with three, and she didn't want another of our family to be admitted. But God who holds the hearts of his creatures in his hand, inclining them to do his will, changed this Sister's disposition. The first one to meet me after my thanksgiving was Sister Aimée, and she called me over to her with a friendly smile and told me to come up with her to your cell. She spoke to me about Céline and there were tears in her eyes. Ah! how many things I have to thank Jesus for; he answers all my requests!

And now I have no other desire except to *love* Jesus unto folly. My childish desires have all flown away. I still love to adorn the Infant Jesus' altar with flowers, but ever since he has given me the *flower* I desired, my *dear Céline,* I desire no other; she is the one that I offer him as my most delightful bouquet.

Neither do I desire any longer suffering or death, and still I love them both; it is *love* alone that attracts me, however. I desired them for a long time; I possessed suffering and believed I had touched the shores of heaven, that the little flower would be gathered in the springtime of her life. Now, abandonment alone guides me. I have no other compass! I can no longer ask for anything with fervor except the accomplishment of God's will in my soul without any creature being able to set obstacles in the way. I can speak these words of the *Spiritual Canticle* of St. John of the Cross:

> In the inner wine cellar
> I drank of my Beloved, and when I went abroad
> Through all this valley
> I no longer knew anything,
> And lost the herd which I was following.
>
> Now I occupy my soul
> And all my energy in his service;
> I no longer tend the herd,
> Nor have I any other work
> *Now that my every act is love.*

> (*Spiritual Canticle,* st. 26 and 28,
> *Collected Works,* p. 413)

Or rather:

After I have known it
love works so in me
That whether things go well or badly
Love turns all to one sweetness
Transforming the soul into itself.

("Without support and with support," *Collected Works,* p. 734f)

How sweet is the way of *love,* dear Mother. True, one can fall or
commit infidelities, but, knowing *how to draw profit from everything,*
love quickly consumes everything that can be displeasing to Jesus; it
leaves nothing but a humble and profound peace in the depths of the heart.

Ah! how many lights have I not drawn from the works of our holy
father, St. John of the Cross! At the ages of seventeen and eighteen I had
no other spiritual nourishment; later on, however, all books left me in
aridity and I'm still in that state. If I open a book composed by a spiritual
author (even the most beautiful, the most touching book), I feel my heart
contract immediately and I read without understanding, so to speak. Or
if I do understand, my mind comes to a standstill without the capacity of
meditating. In this helplessness, holy scripture and the *Imitation* come to
my aid; in them I discover a solid and very *pure* nourishment. But it is
especially the *gospels* which sustain me during my hours of prayer, for
in them I find what is necessary for my poor little soul. I am constantly
discovering in them new lights, hidden and mysterious meanings.

I understand and I know from experience that: *"The kingdom of God
is within you"* (Lk 17:21). Jesus has no need of books or teachers to
instruct souls; he teaches without the noise of words. Never have I heard
him speak, but I feel that he is within me at each moment; he is guiding
and inspiring me with what I must say and do. I find just when I need
them certain lights which I had not seen until then, and it isn't most
frequently during my hours of prayer that these are most abundant but
rather in the midst of my daily occupations.

O my dear Mother! after so many graces can I not sing with the
psalmist: *"How good is the Lord, his mercy endures forever!"* (Ps 117:1).
It seems to me that if all creatures had received the same graces I received,
God would be feared by none but would be loved to the point of folly;
and through *love,* not through fear, no one would ever consent to cause
him any pain. I understand, however, that all souls cannot be the same,
that it is necessary there be different types in order to honor each of God's

perfections in a particular way. To me he has granted his *infinite mercy,*
and *through it* I contemplate and adore the other divine perfections! All
of these perfections appear to be resplendent *with love;* even his justice
(and perhaps this even more so than the others) seems to me clothed in
love. What a sweet joy it is to think that God is *just,* i.e., that he takes into
account our weakness, that he is perfectly aware of our fragile nature.
What should I fear then? Ah! must not the infinitely just God, who deigns
to pardon the faults of the prodigal son with so much kindness, be just
also toward me who "am with him always" (Lk 15:31)?

This year, June 9, the feast of the Holy Trinity, I received the grace to
understand more than ever before how much Jesus desires to be loved.

I was thinking about the souls who offer themselves as victims of
God's justice in order to turn away the punishments reserved to sinners,
drawing them upon themselves. This offering seemed great and very
generous to me, but I was far from feeling attracted to making it. From
the depths of my heart, I cried out:

"O my God! Will your justice alone find souls willing to immolate
themselves as victims? Does not your *merciful love* need them too? On
every side this love is unknown, rejected; those hearts upon whom you
would lavish it turn to creatures seeking happiness from them with their
miserable affection; they do this instead of throwing themselves into your
arms and of accepting your infinite *love.* O my God! Is your disdained
love going to remain closed up within your heart? It seems to me that if
you were to find souls offering themselves as victims of holocaust to your
love, you would consume them rapidly; it seems to me, too, that you
would be happy not to hold back the waves of infinite tenderness within
you. If your justice loves to release itself, this justice *which extends only
over the earth,* how much more does your merciful love desire to *set souls
on fire* since your mercy *reaches to the heavens* (Ps 35:6). O my Jesus,
let me be this happy victim; consume your holocaust with the fire of your
divine love!"

You permitted me, dear Mother, to offer myself in this way to God,
and you know the rivers or rather the oceans of graces which flooded my
soul. Ah! since that happy day, it seems to me that *love* penetrates and
surrounds me, that at each moment this *merciful love* renews me, purifying my soul and leaving no trace of sin within it, and I need have no fear
of purgatory. I know that of myself I would not merit even to enter that
place of expiation since only holy souls can have entrance there, but I also
know that the fire of love is more sanctifying than is the fire of purgatory.

I know that Jesus cannot desire useless sufferings for us, and that he would not inspire the longings I feel unless he wanted to grant them. Oh! how sweet is the way of love! How I want to apply myself to doing the will of God always with the greatest self-surrender!

Here, dear Mother, is all I can tell you about the life of your little Thérèse; you know better than I do what she is and what Jesus has done for her. You will forgive me for having abridged my religious life so much. How will this "story of a little white flower" come to an end? Perhaps the little flower will be plucked in her youthful freshness or else transplanted to other shores.* I don't know, but what I am certain about is that God's mercy will accompany her always, that it will never cease blessing the dear Mother who offered her to Jesus; she will rejoice eternally at being one of the flowers of her crown. And with this dear Mother she will sing eternally the New Canticle of Love.

(Story, VIII)

In the life of the saints, we find many of them who didn't want to leave anything of themselves behind after their death, not the smallest souvenir, not the least bit of writing. On the contrary, there are others, like our holy mother St. Teresa, who have enriched the Church with their lofty revelations, having no fears of revealing the secrets of the King (Tb 12:7) in order that they may make him more loved and known by souls. Which of these two types of saints is more pleasing to God? It seems to me, Mother, they are equally pleasing to him, since all of them followed the inspiration of the Holy Spirit and since the Lord has said: *"Tell the just man all is well"* (Is 3:10). Yes, all is well when one seeks only the will of Jesus, and it is because of this that I, a poor little flower, obey Jesus when trying to please my beloved Mother.

You know, Mother, I have always wanted to be a saint. Alas! I have always noticed that when I compared myself to the saints, there is between them and me the same difference that exists between a mountain whose summit is lost in the clouds and the obscure grain of sand trampled underfoot by the passers-by. Instead of becoming discouraged, I said to

---

* A Carmelite convent had been founded in Saigon from Lisieux in 1861. At this time when Thérèse was writing the Saigon convent was planning a new foundation in Hanoi and had asked the Lisieux convent for some personnel. Thérèse was among those being considered for this project.

myself: God cannot inspire unrealizable desires. I can, then, in spite of my littleness, aspire to holiness. It is impossible for me to grow up, and so I must bear with myself such as I am with all my imperfections. But I want to seek out a means of going to heaven by a little way, a way that is very straight, very short, and totally new.

We are living now in an age of inventions, and we no longer have to take the trouble of climbing stairs, for, in the homes of the rich, an elevator has replaced these very successfully. I wanted to find an elevator which would raise me to Jesus, for I am too small to climb the rough stairway of perfection. I searched, then, in the scriptures for some sign of this elevator, the object of my desires, and I read these words coming from the mouth of eternal Wisdom: *"Whoever is a little one, let him come to me"* (Prv 9:4). And so I succeeded. I felt I had found what I was looking for. But wanting to know, O my God, what you would do to *the very little one* who answered your call, I continued my search and this is what I discovered: *"As one whom a mother caresses, so will I comfort you; you shall be carried at the breasts, and upon the knees they shall caress you"* (Is 66:13, 12). Ah! never did words more tender and more melodious come to give joy to my soul. The elevator which must raise me to heaven is your arms, O Jesus! And for this I had no need to grow up, but rather I had to remain *little* and become this more and more.

O my God, you surpassed all my expectation. I want only to sing of your mercies. "You have taught me from my youth, O God, and until now I will declare your wonderful works. And until old age and grey hairs, O God, forsake me not" (Ps 70:17-18). What will this old age be for me? It seems this could be right now, for two thousand years are not more in the Lord's eyes than are twenty years, than even a single day (Ps 89:4).

Ah! don't think, dear Mother, that your child wants to leave you; don't think she feels it is a greater grace to die at the dawn of the day rather than at its close. What she esteems and what she desires only is *to please* Jesus.

(Story, X)

Ah! it is prayer, it is sacrifice which give me all my strength; these are the invincible weapons which Jesus has given me. They can touch souls much better than words as I have very frequently experienced. There is one among them all which made a sweet and profound impression upon me.

It was during Lent, and I was occupied then with the one and only novice who was here and whose angel I was. She came looking for me one morning, her face radiant with joy, and said: "Ah! if you only knew what I dreamt last night. I was with my sister and wanted to detach her from all the vanities she loves so much. To do this I was explaining this stanza of *Vivre d'Amour:*

> Their loss is gain who all forsake
> To find Thy love, O Jesus mine!
> For Thee my ointment jar I break,
> The perfume of my life is Thine!

"I had a feeling that my words penetrated her soul and I was carried away with joy. This morning when I awoke I thought that God perhaps willed that I give him this soul. May I write her after Lent to tell her about my dream and tell her that Jesus wants her entirely for himself?"

Without giving it much thought, I told her she could try to do this, but first she must ask permission from Mother Prioress. As Lent was still far from coming to a close, you were very much surprised, dear Mother, at the request which appeared too premature; and certainly inspired by God, you answered it was not through letters Carmelites must save souls but through *prayer.*

When I learned of your decision I understood at once it was that of Jesus, and I said to Sister Marie of the Trinity: "We must get to work; let's pray very much. What a joy if we are answered *at the end of Lent!*" Oh! infinite mercy of the Lord, who really wants to answer the prayer of his little children. *At the end of Lent* one more soul was consecrated to Jesus. It was a real miracle, a miracle obtained by the fervor of a humble novice!

How great is the power of *prayer!* One could call it a queen who has at each instant free access to the king and who is able to obtain whatever she asks. To be heard it is not necessary to read from a book some beautiful formula composed for the occasion. If this were the case, alas, I would have to be pitied! Outside the *Divine Office* which I am very unworthy to recite, I do not have the courage to force myself to search out *beautiful* prayers in books. There are so many of them it really gives me a headache! and each prayer is more *beautiful* than the others. I cannot recite them all and not knowing which to choose, I do like children who do not know how to read, I say very simply to God what I wish to say, without composing beautiful sentences, and he always understands me. For me, *prayer* is an aspiration of the heart, it is a simple glance directed to heaven, it is a cry of gratitude and love in the midst of trial as well as joy; finally, it is something great, supernatural, which expands my soul and unites me to Jesus.

(*Story*, XI)

The Fruits of Love

January–December 1896

It was in June 1897 that Thérèse began to write the sequel to her childhood memories at the request of Mother Marie de Gonzague, who had been urged by Mother Agnes to get Thérèse to give her thoughts on religious life.

Thérèse could say on her death-bed: "I have understood humility of heart. . . . It seems to me I'm humble." Now, addressing Mother de Gonzague, she says she is not going to compose beautiful sentences in order to have her believe that she [Thérèse] has a lot of humility. No, she is going to say what great things God has done for her, the greatest of which is to have shown her her littleness, her impotence. Here we have authentic humility, because humility is truth, and there is no greater truth than that of our impotence to do anything without God's grace.

It was on the night of Good Friday-Holy Saturday 1896 that Thérèse had her first hymoptysis. This she looked on as the first call of the Bridegroom, and she was filled with joy at the thought of going to heaven soon. The call was repeated the following night, confirming her imminent entrance into eternal life. But the Bridegroom was not yet satisfied that his bride had the wedding garment he desired for her. Up to now she had a vivid faith, but after Easter the darkness came down and she could appreciate that there were really people who did not believe in God. But she was content to sit at the "table of sinners" in order to make reparation for them. She has no longer the joy of faith but she makes acts of faith and does works which prove her faith. Her one desire is to love to the point of dying of love. Her sufferings bring joy because they are pleasing to God. Even if God should not know of her suffering—which is impossible—she would still be happy to have it if it could make reparation for one single sin against faith. Fear had no place in her life. She had told us already that she recoiled from fear, but with love not only did she advance but she flew. Now she returns to a favorite biblical text: "Can a mother forget her child? . . . Well! even if a mother were to forget her child, I myself will never forget you" (Is 49:15). We are now living under the law of love and we have a spouse who allows himself to be enchained by a hair fluttering on our neck (cf. Sg 4:9).

Thérèse tells us about a dream she had in which three Carmelite nuns appeared to her, among them Venerable Anne of Jesus, Foundress of Carmel in France. It consoled her when Anne gave her a "glance filled with love." Thérèse asked her if God would soon come to take her away and she was told yes, soon, soon. She also wanted to know if God wanted anything more from her and was reassured that: "God asks no other thing of you. He is content, very content."

With her immense desires, Thérèse would have liked to carry out all the vocations possible, and even one form of martyrdom would not satisfy her. It was when she could no longer accept her limitations that she read chapters 12 and 13 of St. Paul's First Letter to the Corinthians. It partly but not fully contented her when she read that there are various parts in the body of the Church, each with its own function. Reading on, she was overjoyed to find that charity was the more excellent way. She had found her vocation. She would be the most vital member of the Church, its heart, without which the other members could not function. Little as she was, she would stay near the throne of the King interceding for her brothers and sisters who carried out the apostolate. But love calls for "works." What works could she do? She would "strew flowers, she will perfume the royal throne with sweet scents, and she will sing in her silvery tones the canticle of love" (*Story*, p. 196).

She wants to use everything to prove her love, "not allowing one little sacrifice to escape, not one look, one word, profiting by all the smallest things and doing them through love." She desires to suffer for love and she will sing while she suffers, "and my song will be all the more melodious in proportion to the length and sharpness of the thorns." She desires to tell all little souls that God would grant them still greater favors than she has received provided they abandoned themselves with total confidence to God's infinite mercy.

Thérèse deliberately chose the contemplative life because she considered this the best way to save souls. She now recalls the fact for Fr. Roulland, her spiritual brother: "I shall be truly happy to work with you for the salvation of souls. It is for this purpose I became a Carmelite nun; being unable to be an active missionary, I wanted to be one through love and penance just like St. Teresa, my seraphic mother," and she assures him "that on the mountain of Carmel a soul is praying unceasingly to the divine Prisoner of Love for the success of your glorious conquest" (Letter 189).

The Arrival of the Spouse

You did not hesitate, dear Mother, to tell me one day that God was enlightening my soul and that he was giving me even the experience of *years*. O Mother! I am *too little* to have any vanity now, I am *too little* to compose beautiful sentences in order to have you believe that I have a lot of humility. I prefer to agree very simply that the Almighty has done great things in the soul of his divine mother's child, and the greatest thing is to have shown her her *littleness*, her impotence.

Dear Mother, you know well that God has deigned to make me pass through many types of trials. I have suffered very much since I was on earth, but, if in my childhood I suffered with sadness, it is no longer in this way that I suffer. It is with joy and peace. I am truly happy to suffer. O Mother, you must know all the secrets of my soul in order not to smile when you read these lines, for is there a soul less tried than my own if one judges by appearances? Ah! if the trial I am suffering for a year now appeared to the eyes of anyone, what astonishment would be felt!

Dear Mother, you know about this trial; I am going to speak to you about it, however, for I consider it as a great grace I received during your office as prioress.

God granted me, last year, the consolation of observing the fast during Lent in all its rigor. Never had I felt so strong, and this strength remained with me until Easter. On Good Friday, however, Jesus wished to give me the hope of going to see him soon in heaven. Oh! how sweet this memory really is! After remaining at the tomb until midnight, I returned to our cell, but I had scarcely laid my head upon the pillow when I felt something like a bubbling stream mounting to my lips. I didn't know what it was, but I thought that perhaps I was going to die and my soul was flooded with joy. However, as our lamp was extinguished, I told myself I should have to wait until the morning to be certain of my good fortune, for it seemed to me that it was blood I had coughed up. The morning was not long in coming; upon awakening, I thought immediately of the joyful thing that I had to learn, and so I went over to the window. I was able to see that I was not mistaken. Ah! my soul was filled with a great consolation; I was interiorly persuaded that Jesus, on the anniversary of his own death, wanted to have me hear his first call. *It was like a sweet and distant murmur which announced the Bridegroom's arrival.*

It was with great fervor that I assisted at Prime and the Chapter of

Pardons. I was in a rush to see my turn come in order to be able, when asking pardon from you, to confide my hope and my happiness to you, dear Mother; however, I added that I was not suffering in the least (which was true) and I begged you, Mother, to give me nothing special. In fact, I had the consolation of spending Good Friday just as I desired. Never did Carmel's austerities appear so delightful to me; the hope of going to heaven soon transported me with joy. When the evening of that blessed day arrived, I had to go to my rest; but just as on the preceding night, good Jesus gave me the same sign that my entrance into eternal life was not far off.

(Story, X)

At the Table of Sinners

At this time I was enjoying such a living faith, such a clear *faith,* that the thought of heaven made up all my happiness, and I was unable to believe there were really impious people who had no faith. I believed they were actually speaking against their own inner convictions when they denied the existence of heaven, that beautiful heaven where God himself wanted to be their eternal reward. During those very joyful days of the Easter season, Jesus made me feel that there were really souls who have no faith, and who, through the abuse of grace, lost this precious treasure, the source of the only real and pure joys. He permitted my soul to be invaded by the thickest darkness, and that the thought of heaven, up until then so sweet to me, be no longer anything but the cause of struggle and torment. This trial was to last not a few days or a few weeks, it was not to be extinguished until the hour set by God himself and this hour has not yet come. I would like to be able to express what I feel, but alas! I believe this is impossible. One would have to travel through this dark tunnel to understand its darkness. I will try to explain it by a comparison.

I imagine I was born in a country which is covered in thick fog. I never had the experience of contemplating the joyful appearance of nature flooded and transformed by the brilliance of the sun. It is true that from childhood I have heard people speak of these marvels, and I know the country in which I am living is not really my true fatherland, and there is another I must long for without ceasing. This is not simply a story invented by someone living in the sad country where I am, but it is a reality, for the King of the fatherland of the bright sun actually came and lived for thirty-three years in the land of darkness. Alas! the darkness did not understand that this divine King was the light of the world (Jn 1:5, 9).

Your child, however, O Lord, has understood your divine light, and she begs pardon for her brothers. She is resigned to eat the bread of sorrow as long as you desire it; she does not wish to rise up from this table filled with bitterness at which poor sinners are eating until the day set by you. Can she not say in her name and in the name of her brothers, *"Have pity on us, O Lord, for we are poor sinners!"* (Lk 18:13). Oh! Lord, send us away justified. May all those who were not enlightened by the bright flame of faith one day see it shine. O Jesus! if it is needful that the table soiled by them be purified by a soul who loves you, then I desire to eat this bread of trial at this table until it pleases you to bring me into your bright kingdom. The only grace I ask of you is that I never offend you!

What I am writing, dear Mother, has no continuity; my little story which resembled a fairy-tale is all of a sudden changed into a prayer, and I don't know what interest you could possibly have in reading all these confused and poorly expressed ideas. Well, dear Mother, I am not writing to produce a literary work, but only through obedience, and if I cause you any boredom, then at least you will see that your little child has given proof of her good will. I am going to continue my little comparison where I left off.

I was saying that the certainty of going away one day far from the sad and dark country had been given me from the day of my childhood. I did not believe this only because I heard it from persons much more knowledgeable than I, but I felt in the bottom of my heart real ongoings for this most beautiful country. Just as the genius of Christopher Columbus gave him a presentiment of a new world when nobody had even thought of such a thing; so also I felt that another land would one day serve me as a permanent dwelling place. Then suddenly the fog which surrounds me becomes more dense; it penetrates my soul and envelops it in such a way that it is impossible to discover within it the sweet image of my fatherland; everything has disappeared! When I want to rest my heart fatigued by the darkness which surrounds it by the memory of the luminous country after which I aspire, my torment redoubles; it seems to me that the darkness, borrowing the voice of sinners, says mockingly to me: "You are dreaming about the light, about a fatherland embalmed in the sweetest perfumes; you are dreaming about the *eternal* possession of the Creator of all these marvels; you believe that one day you will walk out of this fog which surrounds you! Advance, advance; rejoice in death which will give you not what you hope for but a night still more profound, the night of nothingness."

Dear Mother, the image I wanted to give you of the darkness that obscures my soul is as imperfect as a sketch is to the model; however, I don't want to write any longer about it; I fear I might blaspheme; I fear even that I have already said too much.

Ah! may Jesus pardon me if I have caused him any pain, but he knows very well that while I do not have *the joy of faith,* I am trying to carry out its works at least. I believe I have made more acts of faith in this past year than all through my whole life. At each new occasion of combat, when my enemy provokes me, I conduct myself bravely. Knowing it is cowardly to enter into a duel, I turn my back on my adversary without deigning to look him in the face; but I run toward my Jesus. I tell him I am ready to shed my blood to the last drop to profess my faith in the existence of *heaven.* I tell him, too, I am happy not to enjoy this beautiful heaven on this earth so that he will open it for all eternity to poor unbelievers. Also, in spite of this trial which has taken away *all my joy,* I can nevertheless cry out: *"You have given me delight, O Lord, in all your doings"* (Ps 91:5). For is there a *joy* greater than that of suffering out of love for you? The more interior the suffering is and the less apparent to the eyes of creatures, the more it rejoices you, O my God! But if my suffering was really unknown to you, which is impossible, I would still be happy to have it, if through it I could prevent or make reparation for one single sin against *faith.*

My dear Mother, I may perhaps appear to you to be exaggerating my trial. In fact, if you are judging according to the sentiments I express in my little poems composed this year, I must appear to you as a soul filled with consolations and one for whom the veil of faith is almost torn aside; and yet it is no longer a veil for me, it is a wall which reaches right up to the heavens and covers the starry firmament. When I sing of the happiness of heaven and of the eternal possession of God, I feel no joy in this, for I sing simply what I *want to believe.* It is true that at times a very small ray of the sun comes to illumine my darkness, and then the trial ceases for *an instant,* but afterwards the memory of this ray, instead of causing me joy, makes my darkness even more dense.

Never have I felt before this, dear Mother, how sweet and merciful the Lord really is, for he did not send me this trial until the moment I was capable of bearing it. A little earlier I believe it would have plunged me into a state of discouragement. Now it is taking away everything that could be a natural satisfaction in my desire for heaven. Dear Mother, it seems to me now that nothing could prevent me from flying away, for I no longer have any great desires except that of loving to the point of dying of love. June 9.*

(Story, X)

J. M. J. T.

July 12, 1896

Jesus †

Dear little Léonie,

I would have answered your *charming* letter last Sunday if it had been given to me. But we are five, and you know I am the littlest . . . so I run the risk of not seeing the letters until after the others or else not at all. . . . I saw your letter only on Friday, and so, dear little sister, I am not late through my own fault. . . .

If you only knew how happy I am to see you in these good dispositions. . . .

I am not surprised that the thought of death is sweet to you since you no longer hold on to anything on earth. I assure you that God is much better than you believe. He is content with a glance, a sigh of love. . . . As for me, I find perfection very easy to practice because I have understood it is a matter of *taking hold of Jesus by his heart.* . . . Look at a little child who has just annoyed his mother by flying into a temper or by disobeying her. If he hides away in a corner in a sulky mood and if he cries in fear of being punished, his mamma will not pardon him, certainly, not his fault. But if he comes to her, holding out his little arms, smiling, and saying: "Kiss me, I will not do it again," will his mother be able not to press him to her heart tenderly and forget his childish mischief? . . . However, she knows her dear little one *will do it again* on the next

---

* On June 9, 1895, Thérèse had made her Act of Oblation to Merciful Love. By then her last remaining wish had been satisfied—that of Céline's entry into Carmel. Nothing now remained but to "love Jesus unto folly." In her Act of Oblation she asks to become "a martyr to your love, O my God," and that this martyrdom might finally cause her to die. In the present text she also refers to this "dying of love" and so recalls the date of her Act of Oblation, June 9.

occasion, but this does not matter; if he takes her again *by her heart,* he will not be punished. . . .

At the time of the law of fear, before the coming of our Lord, the prophet Isaias already said, speaking in the name of the King of heaven: "Can a mother forget her child? . . . Well! even if a mother were to forget her child, I myself will never forget you" (Is 49:15). What a delightful promise! Ah! we who are living in the law of love, how can we not profit by the loving advances our Spouse is making to us . . . how can we fear him who allows himself to be enchained by *a hair* fluttering on our neck (see Sg 4:9).

Let us understand, then, how to hold him prisoner, this God who becomes the beggar of our love. When telling us that it is a hair that can effect this prodigy, he is showing us that the *smallest actions* done out of love are the ones which charm his heart.

Ah! if we had to do great things, how much we would have to be pitied? . . . But how fortunate we are since Jesus allows himself to be enchained by the *smallest things.* . . .

It is not little sacrifices you lack, dear Léonie, is not your life made up of them? . . . I take delight at seeing you before such a treasure and especially when thinking you know how to profit from it, not only for yourself, but for souls. . . . It is so sweet *to help Jesus* by our light sacrifices, to help him save souls that he bought at the price of his blood and that are awaiting only our help in order not to fall into the abyss. . . .

It seems to me that if our *sacrifices* are the hairs which captivate Jesus, our *joys* are also; for this, it suffices not to center in on a selfish happiness but *to offer* our Spouse the *little joys* he is sowing on the path of life to charm our souls and *raise* them to himself. . . .

I intended writing Aunt today, but I have no time; this will be on next Sunday. I beg you to tell her how much I love her and dear Uncle as well.

I am thinking very often of Jeanne and Francis.

You ask me for some news about my health. Well! dear little sister, I am not coughing anymore. Are you satisfied? . . . This will not prevent God from taking me when he wills; since I am putting forth all my efforts to be a very little child, I have no preparations to make. Jesus himself will have to pay the expenses of the journey and the cost of entering heaven. . . .

Adieu, dear little sister, I love you I believe more and more. . . .

Your little sister,
Thérèse of the Child Jesus
rel. carm. ind.

(L 191, to Léonie)

In the Heart of the Church

J. M. J. T.

September 8, 1896

(To my dear Sister Marie of the Sacred Heart)

O Jesus, my Beloved, who could express the tenderness and sweetness with which you are guiding my soul! It pleases you to cause the rays of your grace to shine through even in the midst of the darkest storm! Jesus, the storm was raging very strongly in my soul ever since the beautiful feast of your victory, the radiant feast of Easter; one Saturday in the month of May, thinking of the mysterious dreams which are granted at times to certain souls, I said to myself that these dreams must be very sweet consolation, and yet I wasn't asking for such a consolation. In the evening, considering the clouds which were covering her heaven, my little soul said again within herself that these beautiful dreams were not for her. And then she fell asleep in the midst of the storm. The next day was May 10, the second *Sunday* of Mary's month, and perhaps the anniversary of the day when the Blessed Virgin deigned to smile upon her little flower.

At the first glimmerings of dawn I was (in a dream) in a kind of gallery and there were several other persons, but they were at a distance. Our Mother was alone near me. Suddenly, without seeing how they had entered, I saw three Carmelites dressed in their mantles and long veils. It appeared to me they were coming for our Mother, but what I did understand clearly was that they came from heaven. In the depths of my heart I cried out: "Oh! how happy I would be if I could see the face of one of these Carmelites!" Then, as though my prayer were heard by her, the tallest of the saints advanced toward me; immediately I fell to my knees. Oh! what happiness! the Carmelite *raised her veil or rather she raised it and covered me with it.* Without the least hesitation, I recognized *Venerable Anne of Jesus,* foundress of Carmel in France. Her face was beautiful but with an immaterial beauty. No ray escaped from it and still, in spite of the veil which covered us both, I saw this heavenly face suffused with an unspeakable gentle light, a light it didn't receive from without but was produced from within.

I cannot express the joy of my soul since these things are experienced but cannot be put into words. Several months have passed since this sweet dream, and yet the memory it has left in my soul has lost nothing of its freshness and heavenly charms. I still see Venerable Mother's glance and smile which was *filled with love*. I believe I can still feel the caresses she gave me at this time.

Seeing myself so tenderly loved, I dared to pronounce these words: "O Mother! I beg you, tell me whether God will leave me for a long time on earth. Will he come soon to get me?" Smiling tenderly, the saint whispered: *"Yes, soon, soon, I promise you."* I added: "Mother, tell me further if God is not asking something more of me than my poor little actions and desires. Is he content with me?" The saint's face took on an expression *incomparably more tender* than the first time she spoke to me. Her look and her caresses were the sweetest of answers. However, she said to me: "God asks no other thing from you. He is content, very content!" After again embracing me with more love than the tenderest of mothers has ever given to her child, I saw her leave. My heart was filled with joy, and then I remembered my sisters, and I wanted to ask her some favors for them, but alas, I awoke!

O Jesus, the storm was no longer raging, heaven was calm and serene. I *believed,* I *felt* there was a *heaven* and that this *heaven* is peopled with souls who actually love me, who consider me their child. This impression remains in my heart, and this all the more because I was, up until then, *absolutely indifferent to Venerable Mother Anne of Jesus.* I never invoked her in prayer and the thought of her never came to my mind except when I heard others speak of her which was seldom. And when I understood to what a degree *she loved me,* how *indifferent* I had been toward her, my heart was filled with love and gratitude, not only for the Saint who had visited me but for all the blessed inhabitants of heaven.

Ah! my Jesus, pardon me if I am unreasonable in wishing to express my desires and longings which reach even unto infinity. Pardon me and heal my soul by giving her what she longs for so much!

To be your *Spouse,* to be a *Carmelite,* and by my union with you to be the *mother* of souls, should not this suffice me? And yet it is not so. No doubt, these three privileges sum up my true *vocation: Carmelite, Spouse, Mother,* and yet I feel within me other *vocations.* I feel the *vocation* of the *warrior, the priest, the apostle, the doctor, the martyr.* Finally, I feel the need and the desire of carrying out the most heroic deeds for *you, O Jesus.* I feel within my soul the courage of the *crusader,* the *papal guard,* and I would want to die on the field of battle in defense of the Church.

I feel in me the *vocation of* the *priest.* With what love, O Jesus, I would carry you in my hands when, at my voice, you would come down from heaven. And with what love would I give you to souls! But alas! while desiring to be a *priest,* I admire and envy the humility of St. Francis of Assisi and I feel the *vocation* of imitating him in refusing the sublime dignity of the *priesthood.*

O Jesus, my love, my life, how can I combine these contrasts? How can I realize the desires of my poor *little soul?*

Ah! in spite of my littleness, I would like to enlighten souls as did the *prophets* and the *Doctors.* I have the *vocation of the apostle.* I would like to travel over the whole earth to preach your name and to plant your glorious cross on infidel soil. But *O my Beloved,* one mission alone would not be sufficient for me, I would want to preach the gospel on all the five continents simultaneously and even to the most remote isles. I would be a missionary, not for a few years only but from the beginning of creation until the consummation of the ages. But above all, O my beloved Savior, I would shed my blood for you even to the very last drop.

Martyrdom was the dream of my youth and this dream has grown with me within Carmel's cloisters. But here again, I feel that my dream is a folly, for I cannot confine myself to desiring *one kind* of martyrdom. To satisfy me I need *all.* Like you, my adorable Spouse, I would be scourged and crucified. I would die flayed like St. Bartholomew. I would be plunged into boiling oil like St. John; I would undergo all the tortures inflicted upon the martyrs. With St. Agnes and St. Cecelia, I would present my neck to the sword, and like Joan of Arc, my dear sister, I would whisper at the stake your name, O *Jesus.* When thinking of the torments which will be the lot of Christians at the time of Anti-Christ, I feel my heart leap with joy and I would that these torments be reserved for me. Jesus, Jesus, if I wanted to write all my desires, I would have to borrow your *Book of Life* (Rv 20:12), for in it are reported all the actions of all the saints, and I would accomplish all of them for you.

O my Jesus! what is your answer to all my follies? Is there a soul more *little,* more powerless than mine? Nevertheless even because of my weakness, it has pleased you, O Lord, to grant my *little childish desires* and you desire, today, to grant other desires that are *greater* than the universe.

During my meditation, my desires caused me a veritable martyrdom, and I opened the Epistles of St. Paul to find some kind of answer. Chapters 12 and 13 of the First Epistle to the Corinthians fell under my eyes. I read there, in the first of these chapters, that *all* cannot be apostles, prophets, doctors, etc., that the Church is composed of different members, and that the eye cannot be the hand *at one and the same time* (see 1 Cor 12: 29, 21). The answer was clear, but it did not fulfill my desires and gave me no peace. But just as Mary Magdalene found what she was seeking by always stooping down and looking into the empty tomb, so I, abasing myself to the very depths of my nothingness, raised myself so high that I was able to attain my end. Without becoming discouraged, I continued my reading, and this sentence consoled me: *"Yet strive after the better gifts, and I point out to you a* yet more excellent way*"* (1 Cor 12:31; 13:1). And the apostle explains how all *the most perfect gifts* are nothing without *love. That charity is the excellent way* that leads most surely to God.

I finally had rest. Considering the mystical body of the Church, I had not recognized myself in any of the members described by St. Paul, or rather I desired to see myself in them *all. Charity* gave me the key to my *vocation.* I understood that if the Church had a body composed of different members, the most necessary and most noble of all could not be lacking to it, and so I understood that the Church *had a heart and that this heart was burning with love. I understood it was love alone that made the Church's members act, that if love* ever became extinct, apostles would not preach the gospel and martyrs would not shed their blood. I understood that *love comprised all vocations, that love was everything, that it embraced all times and places. . . . In a word, that it was eternal!*

Then, in the excess of my delirious joy, I cried out: O Jesus, my love . . . my *vocation,* at last I have found it. . . . *My vocation is love!*

Yes, I have found my place in the Church and it is you, O my God, who have given me this place; in the heart of the Church, my Mother, I shall be *love.* Thus I shall be everything, and thus my dream will be realized.

Why speak of a delirious joy? No, this expression is not exact, for it was rather the calm and serene peace of the navigator perceiving the beacon which must lead him to the port . . . O luminous beacon of love, I know how to reach you, I have found the secret of possessing your flame.

I am only a child, powerless and weak, and yet it is my weakness that gives me the boldness of offering myself as *victim of your love, O Jesus!* In times past, victims, pure and spotless, were the only ones accepted by the strong and powerful God. To satisfy divine *justice,* perfect victims were necessary, but the *law of love* has succeeded to the law of fear, and *Love* has chosen me as a holocaust, me, a weak and imperfect creature.

Is not this choice worthy of *love?* Yes, in order that Love be fully satisfied, it is necessary that it lower itself, and that it lower itself to nothingness and transform this nothingness into *fire.*

O Jesus, I know it, love is repaid by love alone, and so I searched and I found the way to solace my heart by giving you love for love. "Make use of the riches which render one unjust in order to make friends who will receive you into everlasting dwellings" (Lk 16:9). Behold, Lord, the counsel you give your disciples after having told them that "The children of this world, in relation to their own generation, are more prudent than are the children of the light" (Lk 16:8). A child of light, I understood that *my desires of being everything,* of embracing all vocations, were the riches that would be able to render me unjust, so I made use of them *to make friends.* Remembering the prayer of Eliseus to his father Elias when he dared to ask him for his *double spirit* (2 Kgs 2:9), I presented myself before the angels and saints and I said to them: "I am the smallest of creatures; I know my misery and my feebleness, but I know also how much noble and generous hearts love to do good. I beg you then, O blessed inhabitants of heaven, I beg you to *adopt me as your child. To you alone will be the glory* which you will make me merit, but deign to answer my prayer. It is bold, I know; however, I dare to ask you to obtain for me *your twofold spirit."*

Jesus, I cannot fathom the depths of my request; I would be afraid to find myself overwhelmed under the weight of my bold desires. My excuse is that I am a *child,* and children do not reflect on the meaning of their words; however, their parents, once they are placed upon a throne and possess immense treasures, do not hesitate to satisfy the desires of the *little ones* whom they love as much as they love themselves. To please them they do foolish things, even going to the extent of *becoming weak* for them. Well, I am the *child of the Church* and the Church is a queen since she is your Spouse, O divine King of kings. The heart of a child does not seek riches and glory (even the glory of heaven). She understands that this glory belongs by right to her brothers, the angels and saints. Her own glory will be the reflected glory which shines on her Mother's forehead. What this child asks for is love. She knows only one thing: to love you, O Jesus. Astounding works are forbidden to her; she cannot preach the gospel, shed her blood; but what does it matter since her brothers work in her stead and she, *a little child,* stays very close to the *throne* of the King and Queen? She *loves* in her brothers' place while they do the fighting. But how will she prove her *love* since *love* is proved by works? Well, the little child *will strew flowers,* she will perfume the royal throne with their *sweet scents,* and she will sing in her silvery tones the canticle of *love.*

Yes, my Beloved, this is how my life will be consumed. I have no other means of proving my love for you other than that of strewing flowers, that is, not allowing one little sacrifice to escape, not one look, one word, profiting by all the smallest things and doing them through love. I desire to suffer for love and even to rejoice through love; and in this way I shall strew flowers before your throne. I shall not come upon one without *unpetalling* it for you. While I am strewing my flowers, I shall sing, for could one cry while doing such a joyous action? I shall sing even when I must gather my flowers in the midst of thorns, and my song will be all the more melodious in proportion to the length and sharpness of the thorns.

O Jesus, of what use will my flowers be to you? Ah! I know very well that this fragrant shower, these fragile, worthless petals, these songs of love from the littlest of hearts will charm you. Yes, these nothings will please you. They will bring a smile to the Church Triumphant. She will gather up my flowers unpetalled *through love* and have them pass through your own divine hands, O Jesus. And this Church in heaven, desirous of playing with her little child, will cast these flowers, which are now infinitely valuable because of your divine touch, upon the Church Suffering in order to extinguish its flames and upon the Church Militant in order to gain the victory for it!

O my Jesus! I love you! I love the Church, my Mother! I recall that *"the smallest act of pure love is of more value to her than all other works together."* But is *pure love* in my heart? Are my measureless desires only but a dream, a folly? Ah! if this be so, Jesus, then enlighten me, for you know I am seeking only the truth. If my desires are rash, then make them disappear, for these desires are the greatest martyrdom to me. However, I feel, O Jesus, that after having aspired to the most lofty heights of love, if one day I am not to attain them, I feel that I shall have tasted *more sweetness in my martyrdom and my folly* than I shall taste in the bosom of the *joy of the fatherland,* unless you take away the memory of these earthly hopes through a miracle. Allow me, then, during my exile, the delights of love. Allow me to taste the sweet bitterness of my martyrdom.

Jesus, O Jesus, if the *desire* of *loving you* is so delightful, what will it be to possess and enjoy this love?

How can a soul as imperfect as mine aspire to the possession of the plenitude of *love?* O Jesus, *my first and only friend,* you whom I *love uniquely,* explain this mystery to me! Why do you not reserve these great aspirations for great souls, for the *eagles* that soar in the heights?

I look upon myself as a *weak little bird,* with only a light down as covering. I am not an *eagle,* but I have only an eagle's *eyes and heart.* In spite of my extreme littleness I still dare to gaze upon the divine Sun, the Sun of love, and my heart feels within it all the aspirations of an *eagle.*

The little bird wills to *fly* toward the bright Sun which attracts its eye, imitating its brothers, the eagles, whom it sees climbing up toward the divine furnace of the Holy Trinity. But alas! the only thing it can do is *raise its little wings*; to fly is not within its *little* power!

What then will become of it? Will it die of sorrow at seeing itself so weak? Oh no! the little bird will not even be troubled. With bold surrender, it wishes to remain gazing upon its divine Sun. Nothing will frighten it, neither wind nor rain, and if dark clouds come and hide the Star of love, the little bird will not change its place because it knows that beyond the clouds its bright Sun still shines on and that its brightness is not eclipsed for a single instant.

At times the little bird's heart is assailed by the storm, and it seems it should believe in the existence of no other thing except the clouds surrounding it; this is the moment of *perfect joy* for the *poor little weak creature.* And what joy it experiences when remaining there just the same! and gazing at the invisible Light which remains hidden from its faith!

O Jesus, up until the present moment I can understand your love for the little bird because it has not strayed far from you. But I know and so do you that very often the imperfect little creature, while remaining in its place (that is, under the Sun's rays), allows itself to be somewhat distracted from its sole occupation. It picks up a piece of grain on the right or on the left; it chases after a little worm; then coming upon a little pool of water, it wets its feathers still hardly formed. It sees an attractive flower and its little mind is occupied with this flower. In a word, being unable to soar like the eagles, the poor little bird is taken up with the trifles of earth.

And yet after all these misdeeds, instead of going and hiding away in a corner, to weep over its misery and to die of sorrow, the little bird turns toward its beloved Sun, presenting its wet wings to its beneficent rays. It cries like a swallow and in its sweet song it recounts in detail all its infidelities, thinking in the boldness of its full trust that it will acquire in even greater fullness the love of *him* who came to call not the just but sinners (see Mt 9:11). And even if the adorable Star remains deaf to the plaintive chirping of the little creature, even if it remains hidden, well, the little one will remain *wet,* accepting its numbness from the cold and rejoicing in its suffering which it knows it deserves.

O Jesus, your *little bird* is happy to be *weak and little.* What would become of it if it were big? Never would it have the boldness to appear in your presence, *to fall asleep* in front of you. Yes, this is still one of the weaknesses of the little bird: when it wants to fix its gaze upon the divine Sun, and when the clouds prevent it from seeing a single ray of that Sun, in spite of itself, its little eyes close, its little head is hidden beneath its wing, and the poor little thing falls asleep, believing all the time that it is fixing its gaze upon its dear Star. When it awakens, it doesn't feel desolate; its little heart is at peace and it begins once again its work of *love.* It calls upon the angels and saints who rise like eagles before the consuming fire, and since this is the object of the little bird's desire the eagles take pity on it, protecting and defending it, and putting to flight at the same time the vultures who want to devour it. These vultures are the demons whom the little bird doesn't fear, for it is not destined to be their *prey* but the prey of the *Eagle* whom it contemplates in the center of the Sun of love.

O Divine Word! You are the adored Eagle whom I love and who alone *attracts me!* Coming into this land of exile, you willed to suffer and to die in order *to draw* souls to the bosom of the eternal fire of the Blessed Trinity. Ascending once again to the inaccessible Light, henceforth your abode, you remain still in this "valley of tears," hidden beneath the appearances of a white host. Eternal Eagle, you desire to nourish me with your divine substance and yet I am but a poor little thing who would return to nothingness if your divine glance did not give me life from one moment to the next.

O Jesus, allow me in my boundless gratitude to say to you that your *love reaches unto folly.* In the presence of this folly, how can you not desire that my heart leap toward you? How can my confidence, then, have any limits? Ah! the saints have committed their *follies* for you, and they have done great things because they are eagles.

Jesus, I am too little to perform great actions, and my own *folly* is this: to trust that your love will accept me as a victim. My *folly* consists in begging the eagles, my brothers, to obtain for me the favor of flying toward the Sun of love with the *divine Eagle's own wings* (Dt 32:11)!

As long as you desire it, O my Beloved, your little bird will remain without strength and without wings and will always stay with its gaze fixed upon you. It wants to be *fascinated* by your divine glance. It wants to become the *prey* of your love. One day I hope that you, the adorable Eagle, will come to fetch me, your little bird; and ascending with it to the furnace of love, you will plunge it for all eternity into the burning abyss of this love to which it has offered itself as victim.

O Jesus! why can't I tell all *little souls* how unspeakable is your condescension? I feel that if you found a soul weaker and littler than mine, which is impossible, you would be pleased to grant it still greater favors, provided it abandoned itself with total confidence to your infinite mercy. But why do I desire to communicate your secrets of love, O Jesus, for was it not you alone who taught them to me, and can you not reveal them to others? Yes, I know it, and I beg you to do it. I beg you to cast your Divine Glance upon a great number of *little* souls. I beg you to choose a legion of *little* Victims worthy of your *love*!

> The very little Sister Thérèse
> of the Child Jesus
> and the Holy Face,
> unworthy religious of Carmel
>
> (*Story*, IX)

Associated with the Priestly Mission

Ah! the Lord is so good to me that it is quite impossible for me to fear him. He has always given me what I desire or rather he has made me desire what he wants to give me; thus a short time before my trial against the faith began, I was saying to myself: Really, I have no great exterior trials and for me to have interior ones God would have to change my way. I do not believe he will do this, and still I cannot always live in repose as I am now; what means, then, will Jesus find to try me? The answer was not long in coming, and it showed me that the One whom I love is not at a loss as to the means he uses. Without changing my way he sent me the trial which was to mingle a salutary bitterness with all my joys. It is not only when he wished to try me that Jesus makes me feel and desire trials. For a very long time, I had a desire which appeared totally unrealizable to me, that of having *a brother as a priest.* I often thought that had my little brothers not flown away to heaven,* I would have had the happiness of seeing them mount the altar; but since God chose to make little angels of them, I could not hope to see my dream realized. And yet, not only did Jesus grant me the favor I desired, but he united me in the bonds of the spirit to *two* of his apostles, who became my brothers. I wish to recount in detail, dear Mother, how Jesus answered my desire and even surpassed it, since I wanted only *one* priest as a brother to remember me each day at the holy altar.

It was our holy mother St. Teresa who sent me my first little brother as a feast-day gift in 1895. I was in the laundry, very much occupied by my work, when Mother Agnes of Jesus took me aside and read a letter she had just received. It was from a young seminarian, inspired, he said, by St. Teresa of Avila. He was asking for a Sister who would devote herself especially to the salvation of his soul and aid him through her prayers and sacrifices when he was a missionary so that he could save many souls. He promised to remember the one who would become his sister at the holy sacrifice each day after he was ordained. Mother Agnes of Jesus told me she wanted me to become the sister of this future missionary.

Mother, it would be impossible for me to express my happiness. My desire, answered in this unexpected way, gave birth in my heart to a joy which I can describe only as that of a child. I would really have to go back to my childhood days to recapture once more the memory of joys so great that the soul is too little to contain them, and not for years had I experienced this kind of happiness. I felt my soul was renewed; it was as if someone had struck for the first time musical strings left forgotten until then.

I understood fully the obligation I was imposing upon myself and I set to work by trying to redouble my fervor. I must admit that at first I had no consolations for stimulating my zeal. After writing one charming letter filled with noble aspirations in which he thanked Mother Agnes of Jesus, my little brother gave no further sign of life until the following July, except that in November he sent a notice saying he had entered the military service. Dear Mother, it was to you that God reserved the completion of the work already begun. No doubt it is through prayer and

---

* Thérèse's two brothers died in infancy: Marie-Joseph, who was born on September 20, 1866, died on February 14, 1867; Marie-Jean Baptiste was born on December 19, 1867, and died on August 24, 1868. She liked to think that had they lived they would have been priests.

sacrifice that we can help missionaries, but when it pleases Jesus to join two souls for his glory, he permits them to communicate their thoughts from time to time in order to incite each other to love God more. However, the *express permission* of authority is necessary for this, for it seems to me that this correspondence would do more harm than good, if not to the missionary, then at least to the Carmelite because of her type of life which tends to too much self-reflection. Instead of uniting her to God, this exchange of letters (even at long intervals) would occupy her mind, and imagining herself to be doing great marvels, she would be simply procuring useless distraction for herself under the cover of zeal. As for me, it is exactly the same with this matter as with all others, and I feel that if my letters are to do any good they must be written under obedience, and that I should feel repugnance rather than pleasure in writing them. For example, when I interview a novice, I try to do this as a mortification and I refrain from asking questions simply to satisfy my curiosity. If she begins to tell me something interesting and then passes on to something which bores me, without finishing what she was saying, I am very careful not to remind her of the subject she set aside, for it seems to me we can do no good when we seek ourself.

(Story, XI)

J.M.J.T

June 23, 1896
Lisieux Carmel

Jesus †

Reverend Father,
I thought it would please our Good Mother to give her on June 21 for her feast day a corporal and a purificator, along with a pall, that she might have the pleasure of sending them to you for *the 29th.** I owe this reverend Mother the interior joy of being united to you by the apostolic bonds of

---

* Adolphe Roulland, a member of the Paris Foreign Missions, asked the prioress of the Lisieux Carmel, Mother de Gonzague, for a "spiritual sister" who would support his missionary apostolate with her prayers and sacrifices. Thérèse was the one chosen, even though she already had a "spiritual brother" in Maurice Bellière. Père Roulland was ordained a priest on June 28, 1896, and celebrated his first Mass on the 29th. It is to this that Thérèse is referring.

prayer and mortification, so I beg you, Reverend Father, to aid me at the holy altar to pay her my debt of gratitude.

I feel very unworthy to be associated in a special way with one of the missionaries of our adorable Jesus, but since obedience entrusts me with this sweet task, I am assured my heavenly Spouse will make up for my feeble merits (upon which I in no way rely), and that he will listen to the desires of my soul by rendering fruitful your apostolate. I shall be truly happy to work with you for the salvation of souls. It is for this purpose I became a Carmelite nun; being unable to be an active missionary, I wanted to be one through love and penance just like Saint Teresa, my seraphic mother. . . . I beg you, Reverend Father, ask for me from Jesus, on the day he deigns for the first time to descend from heaven at your voice, ask him to set me on fire with his love so that I may enkindle it in hearts.

For a long time I wanted to know an apostle who would pronounce my name at the holy altar on the day of his first Mass. . . . I wanted to prepare for him the sacred linens and the white host destined to veil the King of heaven. . . . The God of Goodness has willed to realize my dream and to show me once again how pleased he is to grant the desires of souls who love him alone.

If I did not fear to be indiscreet, I would ask you, Reverend Father, to make each day at the holy altar a memento for me. . . . When the ocean will separate you from France, you will recall, when looking at the pall which I painted with so much joy, that on the mountain of Carmel a soul is praying unceasingly to the divine Prisoner of love for the success of your glorious conquest.

I want, Reverend Father, our apostolic union to be known only to Jesus, and I beg one of your first blessings for her who will be happy to call herself eternally,

Your unworthy little Sister
in Jesus-Victim,
Thérèse of the Child Jesus
of the Holy face
rel. carm. ind.

(L 189, to P. Adolphe Roulland, of the Foreign Missions)

J. M. J. T.

November 1, 1896

Jesus †

Brother,

Your interesting letter, which arrived under the patronage of All Saints, gives me great joy. I thank you for treating me as a *real sister*. With the grace of Jesus I hope to make myself worthy of this title so dear to me.

I thank you, too, for having sent us *The Soul of a Missionary*; this book has interested me deeply. It allowed me to follow you during your distant journey. The *Life* of Père Nempon is perfectly titled, it really reveals the soul of a missionary, or rather the soul of all apostles truly worthy of this name.

You ask me (in the letter written at Marseilles) to pray to our Lord to remove from you the cross of being named director in a seminary or even that of coming back to France. I understand that this prospect is not pleasing to you; with my whole heart I am begging Jesus that he see fit to allow you to carry out the laborious apostolate such as your soul always dreamed about. However, I add with you: "May God's will be done." In it alone is rest to be found; outside this lovable *will* we would do *nothing* either for Jesus or for souls.

I cannot tell you, Brother, how happy I am to see you so totally abandoned into your superiors' hands. It seems to me it is a certain proof that one day my desires will be realized, that is, that you will be a great saint.

Allow me to confide a secret to you that was just revealed to me by the sheet of paper on which are written the memorable dates of your life.

On September 8, 1890, your missionary vocation was saved by Mary, Queen of Apostles and Martyrs; on that same day, a little Carmelite became the spouse of the King of heaven. Bidding an everlasting *adieu* to the world, she had one goal, to save souls, especially the souls of apostles. From Jesus, her divine Spouse, she asked particularly for an apostolic soul; unable to be a priest, she wanted that in her place a priest may receive the graces of the Lord, that he have the same aspirations, the same desires as herself. . . .

Brother, you know the unworthy Carmelite who offered this prayer. Do you not think, as I do, that our union confirmed on the day of your priestly ordination began on September 8? . . . I believed I would meet only in heaven the apostle, the brother whom I had asked from Jesus; but this beloved Savior, raising a little the mysterious veil that hides the secrets of eternity, has seen fit to give me in this exile the consolation of knowing the brother of my soul, of working with him for the salvation of poor infidels.

Oh! how great is my gratitude when I consider the kind attention of Jesus! . . . What is he reserving for us in heaven if here below his love dispenses surprises so delightful?

More than ever, I understand that the smallest events of our life are conducted by God; he is the one who makes us desire and who grants our desires. . . . When our good Mother suggested to me that I become your helper, I admit, Brother, that I hesitated. Considering the virtues of the holy Carmelites around me, I thought that our Mother would have better served your spiritual interests by choosing for you a Sister other than myself; the thought alone that Jesus would have no regard for my imperfect works but for my good will made me accept the honor of sharing in your apostolic works. I did not know then that our Lord himself had chosen me, he who uses the weakest instruments to work marvels! . . . I did not know that for six years I had *a brother* who was preparing himself to become a missionary; now that this brother is really his apostle, Jesus reveals it to me in order no doubt to increase in my soul the desire of loving him and making him loved.

Do you know, Brother, that if the Lord *continues* to answer my prayer, you will obtain a favor which your humility prevents you from seeking? This incomparable favor, you guess it, is martyrdom. . . .

Yes, I have the hope that after *long years* spent in apostolic works, after having given Jesus love for love, life for life, you will give him, too, blood for blood. . . .

When writing these lines, I am reminded that they will reach you in the month of January, the month during which we exchange happy wishes. I believe that those of your little sister will be the only ones of their kind. . . . To tell the truth, the world would treat as folly wishes like these; however, for us the world no longer lives, and "our conversation is already in heaven" (Phil 3:20), our only desire is to resemble our adorable Master, whom the world did not wish to know because he emptied himself, taking on the form and nature of a slave (see Phil 2:7). Oh, Brother! how blessed you are to follow so closely the example of Jesus. . . . When thinking you have dressed yourself in the clothes of the Chinese, I am naturally thinking of the Savior clothing himself in our poor humanity and becoming like one of us (see Phil 2:7) in order to redeem our souls for eternity.

You will perhaps find me really childish, but it does not matter. I confess that I committed a sin of envy when reading that your hair was going to be cut and replaced by a Chinese braid. It is not the latter I desire but very simply a little tress of the hair now become useless. You will no doubt ask me, laughing, what I will do with it? Well, it is very simple, this hair will be a *relic* for me when you will be in heaven, the palm of martyrdom in your hand. You find, no doubt, that I am going about this far in advance, but I know it is the only means of reaching my goal, for your little sister (who is known only as such by Jesus) will certainly be forgotten in the distribution of *your relics.* I am sure you are laughing at me, but this does not matter. If you consent *to pay* for the little amusement I am giving you with "the hair of a future martyr," I shall be well recompensed.

On December 25 I will not fail to send my angel so that he may place my intentions near the host that will be consecrated by you. It is from the depths of my heart that I thank you for offering for our Mother and me your Mass at dawn; when you are at the altar, we shall be singing Matins for Christmas which precede the Midnight Mass.

Brother, you are not mistaken when saying that no doubt my intentions would be "to thank Jesus for the day of graces among all days." It is not on this day that I received the grace of my religious vocation. Our Lord, willing for himself alone my first glance, saw fit to ask my heart in the cradle, if I can so express myself.

The *night* of Christmas 1886 was, it is true, decisive for my vocation, but to name it more clearly I must call it: the night of my conversion. On that blessed night, about which it is written that it sheds light even on the delights of God himself (see Ps 138), Jesus, who saw fit to make himself a child out of love for me, saw fit to have me come forth from the swaddling clothes and imperfections of childhood. He transformed me in such a way that I no longer recognized myself. Without this change I would have had to remain for years in the world. Saint Teresa, who said to her daughters: "I want you to be women in nothing, but that in everything you may equal strong men," would not have wanted to acknowledge me as her child if the Lord had not clothed me in his divine strength, if he had not himself armed me for war.

I promise you, Brother, to recommend to Jesus in a very special way the young girl about whom you speak to me and who is meeting with obstacles to her vocation. I sympathize sincerely with her suffering, knowing by experience how bitter it is to be unable to respond immediately to God's call. I hope she is not obliged like me to go even to Rome. . . . No doubt you do not know that your sister had the audacity to speak to the pope? . . . It is true, however, and if I had not had this audacity, perhaps I would be still in the world.

Jesus has said: "The kingdom of heaven suffers violence, and only the violent take it away" (Mt 11:12). It was the same for me concerning the kingdom of Carmel. Before becoming the prisoner of Jesus, I had to travel very far to take hold of the prison that I preferred to all the palaces of this earth. I had no desire to make a trip for my personal pleasure, and when my incomparable father offered to take me to Jerusalem if I wished to postpone my entrance for two or three months, I did not hesitate (in spite of the natural attraction which was drawing me to visit the places sanctified by the Savior's life) to choose repose in the shadow of him for whom I was longing. I understood that really one day spent in the Lord's house was worth more than a thousand anywhere else (see Ps 83:11).

Perhaps, Brother, you want to know what obstacle I was encountering in the accomplishment of my vocation; this obstacle was none other than my youth. Our good Father Superior formally refused to receive me before I was twenty-one, saying that a child of fifteen was not capable of knowing to what she was committing herself. His conduct was prudent, and I do not doubt that, in trying me, he accomplished the will of God, who willed to have me conquer the fortress of Carmel at the point of the sword; perhaps, too, Jesus permitted the demon to hinder a vocation which must not have been, I believe, to the liking of that villain *deprived of love* as our holy Mother called him; fortunately, all his tricks turned out to his shame, they served only to render a child's victory more striking. If I wanted to write you all the details of the combat I had to sustain, I would have to have much time, ink, and paper. Recounted by a clever pen, these details would have some interest for you, I believe, but my pen cannot give any charms to a long recital, so I ask your pardon for having already perhaps bored you.

You promise me, Brother, to continue each morning to say at the altar: "My God, enkindle my sister with your love." I am deeply grateful to you for this, and I have no difficulty in assuring you that your conditions are and *always* will be accepted. All I ask Jesus for myself, I ask also for you; when I offer my weak love to the Beloved, I allow myself to offer yours at the same time. Like Joshua, you are fighting on the plain, and I am your little Moses, and incessantly my heart is lifted to heaven to obtain the victory. Oh, Brother, how you would have to be pitied if Jesus himself were not to hold up the arms of your Moses! . . . But with the help of the prayer you are making each day for me to the divine Prisoner of love, I hope you will never have *to be pitied* and that, after this life during which we shall have sown together in tears, we shall be joyful, carrying back our sheaves in our hands (see Ps 125:5-6).

I loved the little sermon very much that you addressed to our good Mother, exhorting her to remain on earth; it is not long, but as you say there is nothing to answer. I see you will not have much trouble in convincing your listeners when you preach, and I hope an abundance of souls will be gathered and offered by you to the Lord. I notice I am at the end of my paper; this forces me to stop my scribbling. I want, however, to tell you that all your anniversaries will be faithfully celebrated by me. *July 3* will be particularly dear to me since on that day you *received Jesus* for the first time and on this same date I *received Jesus* from your hand and assisted at your first Mass in Carmel.

Bless your unworthy sister, Brother.

Thérèse of the Child Jesus
rel. carm. ind.

I recommend to your prayers a young seminarian who would like to be a *missionary*; his vocation has just been shaken by his year of military service.

(L 201, to P. Roulland)

PERIOD FIVE

The Fulfillment of Love

January–September 1897

"I am only a child, powerless and weak, and yet it is my weakness that gives me the boldness of offering myself as *victim* of your love, O Jesus. ... Love has chosen me as a holocaust, me, a weak and imperfect creature" (*Story*, p. 195).

Thérèse was suffering now in her last weeks on earth the most atrocious physical pain and the darkness of faith. In her the theological virtues were coming to perfection. She was love in the heart of the Church; she was undergoing the night of faith, but she was buoyant with hope.

It comes as a surprise to us to hear that it is only now, in the last year of her life, that she has received the grace to understand what charity is (cf. *Story*, p. 219). She had applied herself to loving God and she had not quite grasped how the second commandment of love was like the first. This was what Jesus now taught her. Her love was to be expressed not only in words but in practice, just like Jesus himself. She had to see how and why Jesus loved his disciples. It was not for their natural qualities, and yet he loved them as friends and brothers. He owes them nothing, but he invites them to reign with him, and to make this possible he dies for them.

This charity is a "new" commandment: it is not the "love your neighbor and hate your enemy" of the old Law, but the "love your enemy and pray for those who persecute you" like Jesus did on the cross. It must be a universal love, for "all who are in the house," that is, for everyone. It must not pass judgement, and Thérèse had personal experience of how wrong such judgements can be. It is a love that gives to all who ask and even allows them to take what is ours without hope of return or even gratitude. It must anticipate the needs of others and when forced to refuse a request, it knows how to couch the refusal in such language that the refusal gives more pleasure than if the request were granted. In a word, it is to allow Jesus to love our brothers and sisters in us. His will is to love in us all those he has commanded us to love.

In her letters in the last weeks of her life, Thérèse returns to some of her most cherished spiritual insights. Writing to Fr. Roulland on May 9, 1897, she says: "My way is all confidence and love. I do not understand souls who fear a friend so tender. . . . I know that the Lord is infinitely just; and it is this justice which frightens so many souls that is the object of my joy and confidence. . . . I expect as much from God's justice as from his mercy."

She had always found the answers to her problems in the scriptures, and now she tells Fr. Roulland how helpful she finds them. Learned books only break her head and dry up her heart, but when she takes up the scriptures, "then all seems luminous to me; a single word uncovers for my soul infinite horizons, perfection seems simple to me, I see it is sufficient to recognize one's nothingness and to abandon oneself as a child into God's arms."

She recalls that before her birth her parents were hoping for a son who would be a missionary priest. Their ambition is now fulfilled because she has a missionary "brother," so he is also their son.

Her vision was always of the eternal. Now, again, she refers to this life as an "exile," and she reminds Fr. Roulland that "life is only a day," urging him that they work together for the salvation of souls while this day lasts.

We are inclined to wish that those who are suffering should die quickly so that they be put out of their pain. Thérèse saw things differently: "If I am leaving the field of battle already, it is not with the selfish desire of taking my rest. The thought of eternal beatitude hardly thrills my heart. For a long time, suffering has become my heaven here below." But even in heaven, as she had said so often and now repeats, she will not rest: "I really count on not remaining inactive in heaven. My desire is to work still for the Church and for souls" (Letter 254).

There is, however, one consolation in her going to heaven: "What attracts me to the homeland of heaven is the Lord's call, the hope of loving him finally as I have so much desired to love him, and the thought that I shall be able to make him loved by a multitude of souls who will bless him eternally" (*ibid.*).

The "New" Commandment

This year, dear Mother, God has given me the grace to understand what charity is; I understood it before, it is true, but in an imperfect way. I had never fathomed the meaning of these words of Jesus: *"The second commandment is like the first: you shall love your neighbor as yourself"* (Mt 22:39). I applied myself especially to *loving God,* and it is in loving him that I understood my love was not to be expressed only in words, for: *"It is not those who say: 'Lord, Lord!' who will enter the kingdom of heaven, but those who do the will of my Father in heaven"* (Mt 7:21). Jesus has revealed this will several times or I should say on almost every page of his gospel. But at the last supper, when he knew the hearts of his disciples were burning with a more ardent love for him who had just given himself to them in the unspeakable mystery of his eucharist, this sweet Savior wished to give them *a new commandment.* He said to them with inexpressible tenderness: *"A new commandment I give you that you love one another: that as I have loved you, you also love one another. By this will all men know that you are my disciples,* if you have love for one another" (Jn 13:34-35).

How did Jesus love his disciples and why did he love them? Ah! it was not their natural qualities which could have attracted him since there was between him and them an infinite distance. He was knowledge, eternal wisdom, while they were poor ignorant fishermen filled with earthly thoughts. And still Jesus called them his *friends, his brothers* (Jn 15:15). He desires to see them reign with him in the kingdom of his Father, and to open that kingdom to them he wills to die on the cross, for he said: *"Greater love than this no man has than that he lay down his life for his friends"* (Jn 15:13).

Dear Mother, when meditating upon these words of Jesus, I understood how imperfect was my love for my Sisters. I saw I didn't love them as God loves them. Ah! I understand now that charity consists in bearing with the faults of others, in not being surprised at their weakness, in being edified by the smallest acts of virtue we see them practice. But I understood above all that charity must not remain hidden in the bottom of the heart. Jesus has said: *"No one lights a lamp and puts it under a bushel basket, but on the lamp-stand, so as to give light to all in the house"* (Mt 5:15). It seems to me that this lamp represents charity which must enlighten and rejoice not only those who are dearest to us but *"all who are in the house"* without distinction.

When the Lord commanded his people to love their neighbor as themselves (see Lv 19:18), he had not as yet come upon the earth. Knowing the extent to which each one loved himself, he was not able to ask of his creatures a greater love than this for one's neighbor. But when Jesus gave his apostles a new commandment, his *own commandment* (Jn 15:12), as he calls it later on, it is no longer a question of loving one's neighbor as oneself but of loving him as *he, Jesus, has loved him,* and will love him to the consummation of the ages.

Ah! Lord, I know you don't command the impossible. You know better than I do my weakness and imperfection; you know very well that never would I be able to love my Sisters as you love them, unless *you,* O my Jesus, *loved them in me.* It is because you wanted to give me this grace that you made your *new* commandment. Oh! how I love this new commandment since it gives me the assurance that your will is *to love in me* all those you command me to love!

Yes, I feel it, when I am charitable, it is Jesus alone who is acting in me, and the more united I am to him, the more also do I love my Sisters. When I wish to increase this love in me, and when especially the devil tries to place before the eyes of my soul the faults of such and such a Sister who is less attractive to me, I hasten to search out her virtues, her good intentions; I tell myself that even if I did see her fall once, she could easily have won a great number of victories which she is hiding through humility, and that even what appears to me as a fault can very easily be an act of virtue because of her intention. I have no trouble in convincing myself of this truth because of a little experience I had which showed me we must never judge.

During recreation the portress rang twice; the large workman's gate had to be opened to bring in some trees for the crib. Recreation was not too gay because you were not there, dear Mother, and I thought that if they sent me to serve as third party I would be happy;* at exactly that moment Mother Subprioress told me to go and serve in this capacity, or else the Sister who was at my side. Immediately I began to untie our apron but slowly in order that my companion untie hers before me, for I thought of giving her the pleasure of serving as third party. The Sister who was

---

* It is customary in Carmelite convents for two of the Sisters to accompany any outsider who may enter the enclosure.

replacing the procuratrix was looking at us, and seeing me get up last, she said: "Ah! I thought as much you were not going to gain this pearl for your crown, you were going too slowly."

Certainly, the whole community believed I had acted through selfishness, and I cannot say how much good such a small thing did to my soul, making me indulgent toward the weaknesses of others. This incident prevents me from being vain when I am judged favorably because I say to myself: Since one can take my little acts of virtue for imperfections, one can also be mistaken in taking for virtue what is nothing but imperfection. Then I say with St. Paul: *"To me it is a very small thing to be judged by you, or by man's day, but neither do I judge myself. He that judges me is the Lord"* (1 Cor 4:3-4).

In order that this judgment be favorable or rather that I be not judged at all, I want to be charitable in my thoughts toward others at all times, for Jesus has said: *"Judge not, and you shall not be judged"* (Lk 6:37).

Remembering that *"charity covers a multitude of sins"* (Prv 10:12), I draw from this rich mine which Jesus has opened up before me.

The Lord, in the gospel, explains in what *his new commandment* consists. He says in St. Matthew: *"You have heard that it was said, 'You shall love your neighbor and hate your enemy.' But I say to you, love your enemies . . . pray for those who persecute you"* (Mt 5:43-44). No doubt, we don't have any enemies in Carmel, but there are feelings. One feels attracted to this Sister, whereas with regard to another, one would make a long detour in order to avoid meeting her. And so, without even knowing it, she becomes the subject of persecution. Well, Jesus is telling me that it is this Sister who must be loved, she must be prayed for even though her conduct would lead me to believe that she doesn't love me: *"If you love those who love you, what reward will you have? For even sinners love those who love them"* (Lk 6:32). And it isn't enough to love; we must prove it. We are naturally happy to offer a gift to a friend; we love especially to give surprise; however, this is not charity, for sinners do this too. Here is what Jesus teaches me also: *"Give to everyone who asks of you, and from him who takes away your goods, ask no return"* (Lk 6:30). Giving to all those who *ask* is less sweet than offering oneself by the movement of one's own heart; again, when they ask for something politely, it doesn't cost so much to give, but if, unfortunately, they don't use very delicate words, the soul is immediately up in arms if she is not well founded in charity. She finds a thousand reasons to refuse what is asked of her, and it is only after having convinced the asker of her tactlessness that she will finally give what is asked, and then only *as a favor*; or else she will render a light service which could have been done in one-twentieth of the time that was spent in setting forth her imaginary rights.

Although it is difficult to give to one who asks, it is even more so *to allow one to take what belongs to you, without asking it back.* O Mother, I say it is difficult; I should have said that this *seems* difficult, for *the yoke of the Lord is sweet and light* (see Mt 11:30). When one accepts it, one feels its sweetness immediately, and cries out with the psalmist: *"I have run the way of your commandments when you enlarged my heart"* (Ps 118:32). It is only charity which can expand my heart. O Jesus, since this sweet flame consumes it, I run with joy in the way of *your new commandment.* I want to run in it until that blessed day when, joining the virginal procession, I shall be able to follow you in the heavenly courts, singing your *new canticle* (see Rv 14:3) which must be *love.*

I was saying: Jesus does not want me to lay claim to what belongs to me; and this should seem easy and natural to me since *nothing is mine.* I have renounced the goods of this earth through the vow of poverty, and so I haven't the right to complain when one takes a thing that is not mine. On the contrary, I should rejoice when it happens that I feel the pinch of poverty. Formerly, it seemed to me that I was attached to nothing, but ever since I understood the words of Jesus, I see on occasions that I am very imperfect. For example, in my work of painting there is nothing that belongs to me, I know. But if, when I am preparing for some work, I find that the brushes and the paints are in disorder, if a rule or a penknife has disappeared, patience is very close to abandoning me and I must take my courage in both hands in order to reclaim the missing object without bitterness. We really have to ask for indispensable things, but when we do it with humility, we are not failing in the commandment of Jesus; on the contrary, we are acting like the poor who extend their hand to receive what is necessary for them; if they are rebuked they are not surprised, as no one owes them anything.

Ah! what peace floods the soul when she rises above natural feelings. No, there is no joy comparable to that which the truly poor in spirit experience. If such a one asks for something with detachment, and if this thing is not only refused but one tries to take away what one already has, the poor in spirit follow Jesus' counsel: *"If anyone takes away your coat, let go your cloak also"* (Mt 5:40).

To give up one's cloak is, it seems to me, renouncing one's ultimate rights; it is considering oneself as the servant and the slave of others. When one has left his cloak, it is much easier to walk, to run, and Jesus adds: *"And whoever forces you to go one mile, go two more with him"* (Mt 5:41). Thus it is not enough to give to *everyone who asks*; I must even anticipate their desires, appear to be very much obliged and honored to render service, and if anyone takes something which is for my use, I must not appear to be sorry about this but happy at being *relieved* of it. Dear Mother, I am very far from practicing what I understand, and still the desire alone I have of doing it gives me peace.

I feel that I have explained myself poorly, even more so than on the other days. I made a *kind of discourse* on charity which must have tired you when you were reading it. Pardon me, dear Mother, and remember that at this very moment the infirmarians practice in my regard what I have just written; they don't hesitate to take two thousand paces when twenty would suffice.* So I have been able to contemplate charity in action! Undoubtedly my soul is embalmed with it; as far as my mind is concerned I admit it is paralysed in the presence of such devotedness, and my pen has lost its lightness. In order for me to translate my thoughts, I have to be *like the solitary sparrow*, and this is rarely my lot. When I begin to take up my pen, behold a Sister who passes by, a pitchfork on her shoulder. She believes she will distract me with a little idle chatter: hay, ducks, hens, visits of the doctor, everything is discussed; to tell the truth, this doesn't last a long time, but there is *more than one good charitable Sister,* and all of a sudden another hay worker throws flowers on my lap, perhaps believing these will inspire me with poetic thoughts. I am not looking for them at the moment and would prefer to see the flowers remain swaying on their stems. Finally, fatigued by opening and shutting this famous copybook, I open a book (which doesn't want to stay open) and say resolutely that I shall copy out some thoughts from the psalms and the gospels for the feast of our Mother.** It's very true that I am not sparing in these quotes.

It is not always possible in Carmel to practice the words of the gospel according to the letter. One is obliged at times to refuse a service because

---

* Thérèse was ill at this time and often went to the garden in a wheelchair where she continued her writing.

**Mother Marie de Gonzague who celebrated her feastday on June 21, feast of St. Aloysius Gonzaga.

of one's duties; but when charity has buried its roots deeply within the soul, it shows itself externally. There is such a delightful way of refusing what cannot be given that the refusal gives as much pleasure as the gift itself. It is true that one hesitates less to claim a service from a Sister who is always disposed to oblige but Jesus has said: "... *and from him who would borrow of you, do not turn away*" (Mt 5:42). Thus under the pretext that one would be forced to refuse, one must not stay away from the Sisters who are always in the habit of asking for help. Neither should one be obliging in order to *appear* so or in the hope that another time the Sister whom one obliges will return the service in her turn, for our Lord says again: "*And if you lend to those from whom you hope to receive in return, what merit have you? For even sinners lend to sinners that they may get back in return as much. But do good, and lend, not hoping for anything in return, and your reward shall be great*" (Lk 6:34-35).

Oh, yes! the reward is great, even on this earth; in this way it is only the first step that costs anything. *To lend* without *hoping for anything* appears difficult to nature; one would prefer *to give,* for a thing given no longer belongs to one. When one comes to you and says in a very convincing way: "Sister, I need your help for a few hours, but don't worry, I have Mother's permission, and I *will return* the time you are giving me because I know how rushed you are." Truly, when one knows very well that never will the time one *lends* be ever returned, one would prefer to say: "I give it to you." This would satisfy self-love, for giving is a more generous act than lending, and then we make the Sister feel we don't depend on her services. Ah! how contrary are the teachings of Jesus to the feelings of nature! Without the help of his grace it would be impossible not only to put them into practice but to even understand them.

(Story, X)

"I Am Not Dying, I Am Entering Life"

J. M. J. T.

Carmel of Lisieux, May 9, 1897

Brother,

I received with joy, or rather emotion, the relics you were so kind to send me. Your letter is almost a letter of *au revoir* for heaven. It seemed when I was reading it that I was listening to the account of your forerunners in the apostolate. On this earth, where all changes, one single thing remains, and this is the conduct of the King of heaven regarding his friends. Ever since he has lifted up the standard of the cross, it is under its shadow that all must fight and carry off the victory. Théophane Vénard said: "The whole of a missionary's life is fruitful in the cross"; and again: "To be truly happy we must suffer, and to live we must die."

Brother, the beginnings of your apostolate are marked with the seal of the cross; the Lord is treating you as a privileged one. It is more by persecution and suffering than by brilliant preaching that he wills to make his kingdom firm in souls. You say: "I am still a child who cannot speak." Père Mazel, who was ordained the same day as you, did not know how to speak either; however, he has already taken up the palm. . . .* Oh! how the divine thoughts are above ours! . . . When learning about the death of this young missionary whom I heard named for the first time, I felt drawn to invoke him; I seemed to see him in heaven in the glorious choir of martyrs. I know that in the eyes of men his martyrdom does not bear this name, but in the eyes of God this sacrifice without any glory is not less fruitful than the sacrifices of the first Christians, who confessed their faith before tribunals. Persecution has changed in form, the apostles of Christ have not changed in sentiment, so the divine master would not be able to change his rewards unless it were to increase them in proportion to the glory which was refused them here below.

I do not understand, Brother, how you seem to doubt your immediate entrance into heaven if the infidels were to take your life. I know one must be very pure to appear before the God of all holiness, but I know, too, that the Lord is infinitely just; and it is this justice which frightens so many souls that is the object of my joy and confidence. To be just is not only to exercise severity in order to punish the guilty; it is also to recognize right intentions and to reward virtue. I expect as much from God's justice as from his mercy. It is because he is just that "he is compassionate and filled with gentleness, slow to punish, and abundant in mercy, for he knows our frailty, he remembers we are only dust. As a father has tenderness for his children, so the Lord has compassion on us" (see Ps 102:8)! Oh, Brother, when hearing these beautiful and consoling words

---

* Fr. Mazel, a companion of Fr. Roulland, was assassinated in China on April 1, 1897, thus gaining the palm of martyrdom. The palm was the symbol of victory in pre-Christian times and was taken over by the Christians.

of the prophet-king, how can we doubt that God will open the doors of his kingdom to his children who loved him even to sacrificing all for him, who have not only left their family and their country to make him known and loved, but even desire to give their life for him whom they love. . . . Jesus was very right in saying that there is no greater love than that (see Jn 15:13)! How would he allow himself to be overcome in generosity? How would he purify in the flames of purgatory souls consumed in the fires of divine love? It is true that no human life is exempt from faults; only the Immaculate Virgin presents herself absolutely pure before the divine Majesty. Since she loves us and since she knows our weakness, what have we to fear? Here are a lot of sentences to express my thought, or rather not to succeed in expressing it, I wanted simply to say that it seems to me all missionaries are *martyrs* by desire and will and that, as a consequence, not one should have to go to purgatory. If there remains in their soul at the moment of appearing before God some trace of human weakness, the Blessed Virgin obtains for them the grace of making an act of perfect love, and then she gives them the palm and the crown that they so greatly merited.

This is, Brother, what I think of God's justice; my way is all confidence and love. I do not understand souls who fear a friend so tender. At times, when I am reading certain spiritual treatises in which perfection is shown through a thousand obstacles, surrounded by a crowd of illusions, my poor little mind quickly tires; I close the learned book that is breaking my head and drying up my heart, and I take up holy scripture. Then all seems luminous to me; a single word uncovers for my soul infinite horizons, perfection seems simple to me, I see it is sufficient to recognize one's nothingness and to abandon oneself as a child into God's arms. Leaving to great souls, to great minds the beautiful books I cannot understand, much less put into practice, I rejoice at being little since children alone and those who resemble them will be admitted to the heavenly banquet (see Mt 19:14). I am very happy there are many mansions in God's kingdom (see Jn 14:2), for if there were only the one whose description and road seems incomprehensible to me, I would not be able to enter there. I would like, however, not to be too far from *your mansion*; in consideration of your merits, I hope God will give me the favor of sharing in your glory, just as on earth the sister of a conqueror, were she deprived of the gifts of nature, shares in the honors bestowed on her brother in spite of her own poverty.

The first act of your ministry in China seemed delightful to me. The little soul whose mortal remains you blessed must have indeed smiled at you and promised you her protection as well as those who are dear to you. How I thank you for counting me among them! I am also deeply touched and grateful for your remembrance of my dear parents at Mass. I hope they are in possession of heaven to which all their actions and desires were directed; this does not prevent me from praying for them, for it seems to me these blessed souls receive a great glory from the prayers offered for them and which they can use for other suffering souls.

If, as I believe, my father and mother are in heaven, they must be looking at and blessing the brother whom Jesus has given me. They had so much wanted a missionary son! . . . I have been told that before my birth my parents were hoping their prayer was finally going to be realized. Had they been able to pierce the veil of the future, they would have seen it was indeed through me their desire was fulfilled; since a missionary has become my brother, he is also their son, and in their prayers they cannot separate the brother from his unworthy sister.

You are praying, Brother, for my parents who are in heaven, and I often pray for yours who are still on earth. This is a very sweet obligation for me, and I promise you to be always faithful in carrying it out even if I leave this exile, and even more so perhaps since I shall know better the graces necessary for them; and when their course here below is ended, I shall come to get them in your name and introduce them to heaven. How sweet will be the family life we shall enjoy throughout eternity! While awaiting this blessed eternity that will open up for us in a short time, since life is only a day, let us work together for the salvation of souls. I can do very little, or rather absolutely nothing, if I am alone; what consoles me is to think that at your side I can be useful for something. In fact, zero by itself has no value, but when placed next to a unit it becomes powerful, provided, however, that it be placed on the *right side,* after and not before! . . . That is where Jesus has placed me, and I hope to remain there always, following you from a distance by prayer and sacrifice.

If I were to listen to my heart, I would not end my letter today, but the end of silence is about to ring. I must bring my letter to our good Mother, who is waiting for it. I beg you, then, Brother, to send your blessing to the *little zero* God has placed near you.

> Sister Thérèse
> of the Child Jesus
> of the Holy Face
> rel. carm. ind.

> (L 226, to P. Roulland)

J. M. J. T.

Carmel of Lisieux, July 14, 1897

Jesus †

Brother,

You tell me in your last letter (which pleased me very much): "I am a *baby* who is learning to talk." Well, I, for the last five or six weeks, am a baby too, for I am living only on *milk*; but soon I shall sit down at the heavenly banquet, I shall quench my thirst at the waters of eternal life! When you receive this letter, no doubt I shall have left this earth. The Lord in his infinite mercy will have opened his kingdom to me, and I shall be able to draw from his treasures in order to grant them liberally to the souls who are dear to me. Believe, Brother, that your little sister will hold to her promises, and, her soul, freed from the weight of the mortal envelope, will joyfully fly toward the distant regions that you are evangelizing. Ah! Brother, I feel it, I shall be more useful to you in heaven than on earth, and it is with joy that I come to announce to you my coming entrance into that blessed city, sure that you will share my joy and will thank the Lord for giving me the means of helping you more effectively in your apostolic works.

I really count on not remaining inactive in heaven. My desire is to work still for the Church and for souls. I am asking God for this and I am certain he will answer me. Are not the angels continually occupied with us without their ever ceasing to see the divine face and to lose themselves in the ocean of love without shores? Why would Jesus not allow me to imitate them?

Brother, you see that if I am leaving the field of battle already, it is not with the selfish desire of taking my rest. The thought of eternal beatitude hardly thrills my heart. For a long time, suffering has become my heaven here below, and I really have trouble in conceiving how I shall be able to acclimatize myself in a country where joy reigns without any admixture of sadness. Jesus will have to transform my soul and give it the capacity to rejoice, otherwise I shall not be able to put up with eternal delights.

What attracts me to the homeland of heaven is the Lord's call, the hope of loving him finally as I have so much desired to love him, and the thought that I shall be able to make him loved by a multitude of souls who will bless him eternally.

Brother, you will not have time to send me your messages for heaven, but I am guessing at them, and then you will only have to tell me them in a whisper, and I shall hear you, and I shall carry your messages faithfully to the Lord, to our Immaculate Mother, to the angels, and to the saints whom you love. I will ask the palm of martyrdom for you, and I shall be near you, holding your hand so that you may gather up this glorious palm without effort, and then with joy we shall fly together into the heavenly homeland, surrounded by all the souls who will be your conquest!

Au revoir, Brother; pray very much for your sister, pray for *our Mother,* whose sensitive and maternal heart has much difficulty in consenting to my departure. I count on you to console her.

I am your little sister for eternity,
Thérèse of the Child Jesus
and of the Holy Face
rel. carm. ind.

(L 254, to P. Roulland)

J. M. J. T.

July 26, 1897

Jesus †

Dear little Brother,

How much your letter pleased me! If Jesus has listened to your prayers and prolonged my exile because of them, he has also in his love answered mine, since you are resigned to losing "my presence, my perceptible activity," as you express it. Ah! Brother, allow me to say it: God is reserving for your soul very sweet surprises; you have written, it is "little accustomed to supernatural things," and I, who am not your little sister for nothing, I promise to have you taste after my departure for eternal life the happiness one can find in feeling a friendly soul next to oneself. It will not be this correspondence, more or less distant, always very incomplete, which you seem to long for, but it will be a fraternal conversation that will charm the angels, a conversation that creatures will be unable to reproach since it will be hidden from them. Ah! how good it will seem to me to be freed from these mortal remains that would oblige me, if, *to suppose the impossible,* I were to be with several persons in my dear little Brother's presence, to look upon him as a stranger, one without any meaning for me! . . . I beg you, Brother, do not imitate the Hebrews who missed "the onions of Egypt" (see Nm 11:5); I have for some time served you only too much these vegetables that make one *shed tears* when coming close to them with the eyes when they are still uncooked.

Now I dream of sharing with you "the *hidden* manna . . ." (see Rv 2:17) that the Almighty has promised to give "to the victor." It is precisely because it is *hidden* that this heavenly *manna* attracts you less than "the onion of Egypt"; but I am sure, as soon as I shall be permitted to offer you an entirely spiritual nourishment, you will not miss the one I would have been giving you if I had remained on earth for a long time. Ah! your soul is too great to be attached to any consolations here below. You must live in heaven by anticipation, for it is said: "Where your treasure is, there is your heart also" (Mt 6:21). Is not *Jesus* your *only treasure*? Since he is in heaven, it is there your heart must dwell, and I tell you very simply, dear little Brother, it seems to me it will be easier for you to live with Jesus when I shall be near him forever.

You must know me only imperfectly to fear that a detailed account of your faults may diminish the tenderness I have for your soul! Oh, Brother, believe it, I shall have no need "to place my hand on the lips of Jesus." He has forgotten your infidelities now for a long time; only your desires for perfection are present to give joy to his heart. I beg you, do not *drag* yourself any longer to *his feet*; follow that "first impulse that draws you into his arms." That is where your place is, and I have learned, more so than in your other letters, that you are *forbidden* to go to heaven by any other way except that of your poor little sister.

I am in total agreement with your opinion: "The divine heart is more saddened by the thousand little indelicacies of his friends than by even the grave sins that persons of the world commit"; but, dear little Brother, it seems to me that it is *only* when his own, unaware of their continual indelicacies, make a habit of them and do not ask his pardon, that Jesus can say these touching words which are placed for us in his mouth by the Church during Holy Week: "These wounds you see in my hands are the ones I received in the house of those who *loved me!*" (Zec 13:6). Regarding those who *love* him and who come after each indelicacy to ask his pardon by throwing themselves into his arms, Jesus is thrilled with joy. He says to his angels what the father of the prodigal son said to his servants: "Clothe him in his best robe, and place a ring on his finger, and let us rejoice." Ah! how little known are the *goodness,* the *merciful love* of Jesus, Brother! . . . It is true, to enjoy these treasures one must humble oneself, recognize one's nothingness, and that is what many souls do not want to do; but, little Brother, this is not the way you act, so the way of simple and loving confidence is really made for you. I would like you to be *simple* with God, but also . . . with me. You are surprised at my sentence? It is because, dear little Brother, you ask my *pardon* "for your *indiscretion,*" which consists in desiring to know if in the world *your sister* was named Geneviève; I find the request very natural, and to prove it to you, I am going to give you some details on my family, for you have not been very well informed.

God gave me a father and a mother more worthy of heaven than of earth; they asked the Lord to give them many children and to take them for himself. This desire was answered: four little angels flew away to heaven, and five children left in the arena took Jesus for Bridegroom. It was with a heroic courage that my father, like a new Abraham, climbed *three times* the mountain of Carmel to immolate to God what was most dear to him. First, there were his two eldest; then the third of his daughters, on the advice of her director and conducted by our incomparable father, made an attempt in the convent of the Visitation. (God was content with her acceptance, *later* she returned to the world where she lives as though in the cloister.) There remained to the elect of God only two children, one eighteen years old, the other fourteen. The latter, "the little Thérèse," *asked permission to fly to Carmel, which she obtained from her good father, who pushed his condescension even to taking her first to Bayeux, then to Rome, in order to remove the obstacles which were holding back the immolation of her whom he called his queen. When he had brought her to port, he said to the only child* who remained with him: "If you want to follow the example of your sisters, I consent to it, do not worry about me." The angel who was to support the old age of such a saint answered that, *after his departure for heaven,* she would also fly to the cloister, which filled with joy him who lived only for God. But such a beautiful life was to be crowned by a trial worthy of it. A short time after my departure, the father whom we cherished with such good reason was seized with an attack of paralysis in his limbs, which was repeated several times, but it could not remain there, the trial would have been too sweet, for the heroic patriarch had offered himself as a victim to God; so the paralysis, changing its course, settled in the venerable head of the victim whom the Lord had accepted. . . . I lack the space to give you some touching details. I want only to tell you that we had to drink the chalice to its very dregs and to separate ourselves for three years from our venerated father, entrusting him to religious but strange hands. He accepted this trial, the entire humiliation of which he understood, and he pushed heroism even to not willing that we ask for his cure.

A *Dieu,* dear little Brother; I hope to write you again if the trembling of my hand does not increase, for I was obliged to write my letter on several occasions. Your little Sister, not *"Geneviève" but "Thérèse"* of the Child Jesus of the Holy Face.

(L 261, to l'abbé Belliére)

J. M. J. T.

Carmel of Lisieux, August 10, 1897

Jesus †

Dear little Brother,

I am now all ready to leave; I received my passport for heaven, and my dear father is the one who obtained this grace for me. On the 29th he gave me the assurance that I was soon to join him; the next day, the doctor, surprised at the progress the sickness had made in two days, told our good Mother that it was time to grant my desires by having me receive extreme unction. I had this happiness, then, on the 30th, and also that of seeing Jesus-Victim leave the tabernacle for me, whom I received as *Viaticum* for my *long* voyage! . . . This bread of heaven fortified me; see, my pilgrimage seems to be unable to end. Far from complaining about it, I rejoice that God permits me to suffer still for his love; ah! how sweet it is to abandon oneself into his arms without fear or desire.

I admit to you, little Brother, that we do not understand heaven in the same way. It seems to you that sharing in the justice, in the holiness of God, I would be unable as on earth to excuse your faults. Are you forgetting, then, that I shall be sharing also in the *infinite mercy* of the Lord? I believe the blessed have great compassion on our miseries, they remember, being weak and mortal like us, they committed the same faults, sustained the same combats, and their fraternal tenderness becomes greater than it was when they were on earth, and for this reason, they never cease protecting us and praying for us.

Now, dear little Brother, I must speak to you about the *inheritance* you will receive after my death. Here is the share our Mother will give you: i) the relic I received on the day of my reception of the habit, and it has never left me since then; ii) a little crucifix which is incomparably more dear to me than the large one, for the one I have now is no longer the first one I had been given. In Carmel, we exchange objects of piety at times; this is a good way to prevent us from becoming attached to them. I return to the little crucifix. It is not beautiful; the face of Christ has almost disappeared. You will not be surprised at this when you realize that since the age of thirteen this souvenir from one of my sisters has followed me everywhere. It was especially during my trip to Italy that this crucifix became precious to me; I touched it to all the famous relics I had the happiness to venerate, and to tell you the number would be impossible for me. Furthermore, it was blessed by the Holy Father. Ever since my illness, I hold our dear little crucifix almost always in my hands; when looking at it, I think with joy that, after having received my kisses, it will go to claim those of my little Brother. Here, then, is what your *inheritance* consists of, and in addition our Mother will give you the *last* picture that I have painted. I am going to end, dear little Brother, where I should have begun, by thanking you for the *great pleasure* you gave me in sending your photograph.

A *Dieu,* dear little Brother; may he give us the grace to love him and save souls for him. This is the wish that your unworthy little Sister Thérèse of the Child Jesus of the Holy Face has.

r.c.i.

(It is by choice that I became your sister.)

(L 263, to l'abbé Bellière)

An Offering to the Merciful Love of God

J. M. J. T.

Offering of Myself as a Victim of Holocaust
to God's Merciful Love

O My God! Most Blessed Trinity, I desire to *love* you and make you *loved,* to work for the glory of the holy Church by saving souls on earth and liberating those suffering in purgatory. I desire to accomplish your will perfectly and to reach the degree of glory you have prepared for me in your kingdom. I desire, in a word, to be a saint, but I feel my helplessness and I beg you, O my God! to be yourself my *sanctity*!

Since you loved me so much as to give me your only Son as my savior and my spouse, the infinite treasures of his merits are mine. I offer them to you with gladness, begging you to look upon me only in the face of Jesus and in his heart burning with *love.*

I offer you, too, all the merits of the saints (in heaven and on earth), their acts of *love,* and those of the holy angels. Finally, I offer you, *O Blessed Trinity!* the *love* and merits of the *Blessed Virgin, my dear Mother.* It is to her I abandon my offering, begging her to present it to you. Her divine Son, my *beloved* Spouse, told us in the days of his mortal life: *"Whatsoever you ask the Father in my name he will give it to you"* (Jn 16:23)! I am certain, then, that you will grant my desires; I know, O my God! that *the more you want to give, the more you make us desire.* I feel in my heart immense desires and it is with confidence I ask you to come and take possession of my soul. Ah! I cannot receive holy communion as often as I desire, but, Lord, are you not *all-powerful*? Remain in me as in a tabernacle and never separate yourself from your little victim.

I want to console you for the ingratitude of the wicked, and I beg of you to take away my freedom to displease you. If through weakness I sometimes fall, may your *divine glance* cleanse my soul immediately, consuming all my imperfection like the fire that transforms everything into itself.

I thank you, O my God! for all the graces you have granted me, especially the grace of making me pass through the crucible of suffering. It is with joy I shall contemplate you on the last day carrying the scepter of your cross. Since you deigned to give me a share in this very precious cross, I hope in heaven to resemble you and to see shining in my glorified body the sacred stigmata of your passion.

After earth's exile, I hope to go and enjoy you in the fatherland, but I do not want to lay up merits for heaven. I want to work for your *love alone* with the one purpose of pleasing you, consoling your sacred heart, and saving souls who will love you eternally.

In the evening of this life, I shall appear before you with empty hands, for I do not ask you, Lord, to count my works. All our justice is stained in your eyes. I wish, then, to be clothed in your own *justice* and to receive from your *love* the eternal possession of *yourself*. I want no other *throne*, no other *crown* but *you*, my *Beloved!*

Time is nothing in your eyes, and a single day is like a thousand years. You can, then, in one instant prepare me to appear before you.

In order to live in one single act of perfect love, *I offer myself as a victim of holocaust to your merciful love*, asking you to consume me incessantly, allowing the waves of *infinite tenderness* shut up within you to overflow into my soul, and that thus I may become a *martyr* of your *love, O* my God!

May this martyrdom, after having prepared me to appear before you, finally cause me to die and may my soul take its flight without any delay into the eternal embrace of *your merciful love.*

I want, O my *Beloved,* at each beat of my heart to renew this offering to you an infinite number of times, until the shadows having disappeared I may be able to tell you of my *love* in an *eternal face to face!*

Marie, Françoise, Thérèse
of the Child Jesus
and the Holy Face,
unworthy Carmelite religious.

This 9th day of June,
Feast of the Most Holy Trinity,
In the year of grace, 1895

CHRONOLOGY

1873   2 January. Birth of Marie-Francoise-Thérèse Martin at Alençon.
          4 January. Thérèse is baptized in the church of Notre-Dame.

1875   First signs of her religious vocation.

1877   18-23 June. Pilgrimage of Thérèse's mother, Mme. Martin, and her sisters Marie, Pauline, and Léonie to Lourdes.
          28 August. Mme. Martin dies. Thérèse chooses Pauline as second mother.
          15-16 November. Thérèse and her sisters arrive at Lisieux.

1881   3 October. Thérèse enters Benedictine Abbey as a day-boarder.

1882   2 October. Pauline enters Lisieux Carmel.

1883   6 April. Pauline receives the habit (Sister Agnes of Jesus).

1884   8 May. Thérèse's first communion at the Abbey; profession of Sister Agnes of Jesus at Carmel.
          14 June. Thérèse's confirmation by Bishop Hugonin, bishop of Bayeux.

1886   15 October. Entrance of Marie to the Lisieux Carmel.
          25 December. After Midnight Mass, grace of conversion.

1887   19 March. Marie receives the habit (Sister Marie of the Sacred Heart).
          1 May. Thérèse's father, M. Martin, has an attack of paralysis.
          29 May (Pentecost). Thérèse receives permission from her father to enter Carmel at only fifteen years of age.
          13 July. The assassin Pranzini is condemned to death. Thérèse prays and makes sacrifices for his conversion.
          1 September. Thérèse reads in the *La Croix* the account of Pranzini's conversion and execution.
          31 October. Visit to Bishop Hugonin at Bayeux to solicit the authorization to enter Carmel.
          20 November. Audience with Leo XIII. Thérèse presents her petition to the pope.
          28 December. Favorable answer from Bishop Hugonin to the prioress to admit Thérèse.

1888   9 April. Thérèse enters the Lisieux Carmel.

        12 August. New attack of paralysis on M. Martin.

1889   5-10 January. Retreat for the reception of the habit.

        10 January. Thérèse receives the habit. M. Martin's last celebration.

1890   8 September. Profession.

1892   12 May. M. Martin's last visit to the Carmel.

1893   20 February. Election of Mother Agnes as prioress. Thérèse is associated in the spiritual formation of her companions in the novitiate.

1894   29 July. M. Martin dies.

        14 September. Entrance of Céline to the Carmel; she is entrusted to Thérèse.

        December. Thérèse receives from Mother Agnes of Jesus the order to write her childhood memories.

1895   During this year she writes Manuscript A.

        5 February. Céline receives the habit (Sister Geneviève).

1896   24 February. Profession of Sister Geneviève.

        Good Friday-Holy Saturday. First hymoptysis.

        5 April (Easter Sunday). Sudden entrance into the Night of Faith, a trial which will last until her death.

        8 September. Thérèse writes Manuscript B (addressed to Sr. Marie of the Sacred Heart).

1897   25 March. Profession of Sister Marie of the Eucharist.

        6 April. Beginning of the last conversations.

        3 June. Mother Marie de Gonzague orders Thérèse to continue her autobiography. Thérèse writes Manuscript C.

        19 August. Receives communion for the last time.

        30 September. Around 7:30 P.M., Thérèse dies after an agony of two days.

        4 October. She is buried in the Lisieux cemetery.

Also available from New City Press:

THE PRAYERS OF ST. JOHN OF THE CROSS
Alphonse Ruiz, O.C.D. (ed.)

From the testimony of those who at one time or another found Saint John entranced in prayer, it can be easily concluded that prayer was something connatural to him. In fact, prayer was such an intimate and solid experience that it occupied his whole life and being. There were times when the strength of his intimate relationship with the Lord gave vent to his personal prayer which we find scattered throughout his writings. These fragments are traced in the present collection which shows the width and depth of Saint John's prayer. Thus we can learn from the saint's experience by enjoying and listening to his vibrant and everlasting words.

Series: "Profiles"
ISBN 0-911782-91-5, paper, 128 pp.

THE PRAYERS OF ST. TERESA OF AVILA
Thomas Alvarez, O.C.D. (ed.)   *2d printing*

"Fr. Alvarez has gathered together the written prayers of St. Teresa, using many of her works. The prayers are deeply personal and introduce the reader to the school of prayer which St. Teresa taught her followers. Fr. Alvarez's commentary is often illuminating."

New Heaven/New Earth

"We have all been somewhat embarrassed by the utterances of those in love. But if the one so afflicted is a poet, as Teresa is, what you get is poetry, or perhaps music. One feels almost shy reading these words, as if one has come unannounced upon lovers. . . . Truly a classic."

New Oxford Review

Series "Profiles"
ISBN 0-911782-76-1, paper, 136 pp.

IN SEARCH OF GOD

by W. Herbstrith (with Teresa of Avila, John of the Cross, Therese of Lisieux, Edith Stein)   *2d printing*

"Herbstrith's message is not that mysticism is easy, but simply that the way of mysticism is open to everyone. . . . Her study of this quartet of Carmelite saints is a vital word on silent prayer and on a spirituality of belief. The theology is lucid and the biographies are simple, together opening up a beautiful mystical path through the forest of ordinary experience."   *B.C. Catholic*

"[The author] writes to 'present ideas that stem from a tradition of Christian meditation' shared by the four Carmelite heroes. An introduction to the four, this book might be helpful to those who want to begin to 'stress the fact that mystical life means to abandon oneself to the closeness of our living God.' "   *National Catholic Reporter*

"This is a helpful primer on spiritual life. . . ."   *Spectrum Review*

Series "Spirituality"
ISBN 0-911728-69-9, paper, 128 pp.

FROM ASH TO FIRE—A Contemporary Journey through the Interior Castle of Teresa of Avila

by Carolyn Humphreys

"Very interesting and useful. Its greatest appeal is the way the author, at every stage of the interior journey, describes the emotions, psychological attitudes and behavior which accompany that stage. The reader will recognize him or herself in many of these profiles, and be urged to move ahead, or at least understand what is happening in one's own life so as to see it as part of God's plan. The book has a very positive thrust. There is an integration of the spiritual into the whole of one's development."
                    Rev. Eugene Selzer, St. Louis, MO

"St. Teresa has inspired many books of commentary and I think Humphrey's book ranks with some of the best literary efforts of this era."
                    S. Schulein, O.C.D.S., Long Beach, CA

Series: "Spirituality"
ISBN 1-56548-012-0, paper, 160 pp.